Crafting
Expository Papers

Crafting Expository Papers

Susan Koehler

Crafting Expository Papers

Cover and Book Design | Hank McAfee

Layout | Mickey Cuthbertson

Library of Congress Cataloging-in-Publication Data

Koehler, Susan, 1963-
Crafting expository papers / Susan Koehler.
p. cm.
Includes bibliographical references.
ISBN-13: 978-0-929895-39-0 (pbk.)
ISBN-10: 0-929895-39-8 (pbk.)
1. Exposition (Rhetoric) 2. English language--Rhetoric--Problems, exercises, etc. 3. Report writing--Problems, exercises, etc. I. Title.

PE1429.K64 2007
808'.066--dc22
2007008509

ISBN-13: 978-0-929895-39-0
ISBN-10: 0-929895-39-8

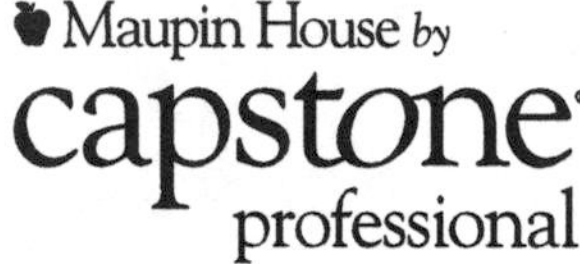

Maupin House Publishing, Inc. by Capstone Professional.
1710 Roe Crest Drive
North Mankato, MN 56003
800-524-0634
352-373-5546 (fax)
www.maupinhouse.com
info@maupinhouse.com

Publishing Professional Resources that Improve Classroom Performance
Printed in the United States of America in Eau Claire, Wisconsin.
102014 008583R

All that I am or ever hope to be

I owe to my angel Mother.

— Abraham L incoln

For my mother

CONTENTS

CONTENTS (continued)

CONTENTS (continued)

Acknowledgements

My heartfelt appreciation goes to Penny C. Brinson, principal of Hawks Rise Elementary School in Tallahassee, Florida. For years she has been an inspiration, committed to positive interactions and outcomes. Her diligent leadership in providing professional development led me to all I have learned about CraftPlus.

I am indebted to Marcia S. Freeman, Julia Graddy, Mark Devish, and all of the great people at Maupin House Publishing. They are dedicated to supporting teachers and learners with high-quality educational materials and customized professional development.

I am grateful to Lana Middlebrooks, a wonderful high school English teacher who remains dedicated to providing her students with a quality liberal arts education. She was so kind to share her ideas and methods with me.

I am so indebted to the many children who have shared their writing with me across many years of teaching. I have learned so much from them.

Finally, I want to thank my dear family for their patience, support, and grounding.

Preface

The writing process is what writers do; writing craft is what writers know.
Marcia S. Freeman

During my twenty-one years in the classroom, I've seen writing instruction evolve from being periodically given story starters and reports to being a fully integrated, regularly assessed staple of modern curricula. And while teaching methods and assessment techniques have changed, one thing has remained constant: the importance of writing craft.

Craft is the element that separates mediocre writing from good writing. Some students have a talent for craft and develop it naturally. But for many students, the key to good writing has remained unintuitive and out of reach.

When testing and accountability entered the picture, the common instructional response was to teach organization and structure. As a result, students' writing developed a tendency to sound stilted and formulaic. There was a need for explicit craft instruction.

Enter CraftPlus®. The CraftPlus curriculum provides the structure and content needed to teach craft explicitly, and allows students to flourish in the writing process. Teachers and students participate in prewriting activities, writers' workshop, peer conferences, author's chair, and individual student-teacher conferences.

This book addresses the genre of expository writing, which is the vast majority of the type of writing students will be required to compose throughout their lifetimes. As with the entire CraftPlus curriculum, Target Skills®—specific writing conventions and literacy techniques that help students master and understand writing craft—are presented through literature models, taught explicitly in mini-lessons, practiced in daily writers' workshop, and refined during response time. For those unfamiliar with the CraftPlus curriculum, there is a brief description of its principles and practices in Appendix A (see page 84).

The skills and methods presented in this book are very specific. However, the models and topics are merely suggestions. Please be sure to make all writing experiences meaningful for your students by selecting topics of high interest and allowing self-selected topics. Integrate your curricula whenever possible.

When you integrate writing with content-area topics of study, you build writing skills in a purposeful way, provide students with something to write about, and reinforce skills taught in the content areas. Additionally, the expository writing skills taught and practiced during this unit of study will support your students in non-fiction reading comprehension.

Remember, the language processes of reading and writing are inseparable partners. As you build your students' abilities to write meaningful expository pieces, you will inadvertently build their reading comprehension as well. Information showing the links between the writing skills and processes taught in this book and expository reading skills and processes can be found on page 2.

As students begin to develop writing-craft skills, their writing becomes more thoughtfully organized, more focused on details, and more enjoyable to read. The key to good writing will be in their hands.

Susan Koehler
February 2007

CHAPTER ONE

Introduction to Teaching Expository Writing

> The Significance of Expository Writing

Expository writing is without a doubt the type of writing that most effectively prepares students for success in school and in the real world. All writing is significant, but expository writing is essential.

By teaching your students to become proficient in this genre, you will empower them to craft well-organized written responses on subject-area assessments and standardized tests. You will prepare them to write well-supported reports and term papers. You will be guiding future professionals in writing legal briefs, communicating processes, and documenting case studies. Your students *will* be required to communicate effectively through expository writing. Therefore, you must meet the challenge of teaching them expository craft.

Teaching the specific craft skills associated with expository writing impacts students in other ways. Becoming a proficient writer is often the first step in becoming a proficient reader. Because an overwhelming percentage of the reading students will be required to do in content-area classes and in their future careers will be non-fiction, it is imperative that they develop skills for comprehending this type of material. Students who learn the nuances of crafting expository *writing* will recognize and comprehend that craft while *reading*. They will be aware of the types of supporting details used, will identify main ideas, and will recognize the organizational structure used in the informational writing they read.

See page 2 for a list of the corresponding reading and writing skills built in this text.

> Expository Defined

Simply put, expository writing informs, explains why, or tells how. A magazine article that informs the reader about the migratory patterns of the Canada goose is informational expository. An editorial column that, using facts, statistics, and examples, explains why a city ordinance needs to be enacted is expository writing intended to persuade the reader with supporting details. A paper that details the steps to correctly conducting a scientific experiment is expository writing intended to communicate a process. As Marcia Freeman says in *Building a Writing Community*, "Expository writing is a genre characterized by information, ideas, opinions, directions, explanations, and argument—all supported by substantive details."

The Reading-Writing Connection

Writing Skill	Corresponding Reading Skill
Prewriting, listing, planning	Activating prior knowledge
"Don't Hit Your Reader over the Head"	Making inferences
Paragraph structures	Main idea and supporting details
Comparison paragraphs	Comparison/contrast
Graphic organizers	Identifying organization and structure in expository text
Sentence building	Sentence comprehension
Using literary devices	Comprehension of imagery
Author's chair	Oral reading fluency and active listening
Establishing purpose and focus	Identifying purpose and focus
Paraphrasing	Summarizing
Discussion groups	Metacognition
Planning and writing a process paper	Sequencing
Cause-and-effect paragraph	Cause and effect

> Expository Papers

The effectiveness of expository papers hinges on two key ingredients: organization and support. The traditional structure of expository writing is the classic three-point, five-paragraph paper. The first paragraph provides the thesis statement and lays out the sub-topics to be addressed; the second, third, and fourth paragraphs provide details to support each sub-topic; and the final paragraph recaps the main points and reiterates the thesis statement. While this classic organizational structure is effective and sometimes required of students, variations of this model stimulate interest by creating a more engaging, less predictable experience for the reader.

In the CraftPlus method, you are encouraged to teach students that the function of the introductory paragraph is to hook the reader's attention and introduce the topic with a thesis statement. Introduction of sub-topics can be reserved for the body of the paper. You can teach your students a variety of techniques for introductions and conclusions that will make a lasting impression on the reader. You can teach them to develop a wealth of supporting details that are specific in nature and varied in presentation. By analyzing expository texts and different types of support, you can help students recognize, learn, practice, and apply meaningful kinds of supporting details. Students can also learn strategies for writing conclusions that are pleasing to the reader and close the writing in a satisfying, thought-provoking way.

Opportunities to practice expository writing occur naturally when you integrate the curriculum with your writing-craft instruction: *Write to inform the reader about the life cycle of a Monarch Butterfly. Write to explain how the invention of the cotton gin impacted the lives of planters and slaves. Write to explain why it is important to follow the Food Guide Pyramid.* You will find that the skills specific to good expository compositions can be taught and practiced across the curriculum.

> Teaching Expository Writing

Instruction in expository writing must extend beyond the assignment of numerous prompts to which students respond and are assessed. To be successful, individual writing-craft skills must be explicitly taught, practiced, applied, and assessed.

Throughout this unit, one of your tasks is to provide models of expository writing and draw attention to the skills employed by the writer. Teachers traditionally rely on fiction for read-alouds in the classroom, but including stimulating non-fiction on a regular basis not only enhances the curriculum, it also presents models of well-crafted expository writing that will raise awareness in young writers. Many non-fiction magazine articles for young readers begin with clever hooks—opening lines that grab the reader's attention and lure them into reading the article. Hooks can be as simple as a compelling question with which the reader can identify, as gripping as a startling fact that will focus the reader, or as attractive as a narrative vignette that pulls the reader into an expository piece. Professional writers use creative hooks that provide excellent models for students.

Beyond hooks, young writers must learn what it takes to support a thesis statement: details. Rather than just expanding and explaining their subtopics in body paragraphs, students can use varied, specific types of supporting details to add concrete validation and convincing evidence. Too often, we advise students to add more support when they don't know exactly *what* to add. The best tool we can give young writers toward improving the quality of expository writing is to teach them how to develop strong supporting details and link them with transitions that create a smooth flow.

The methods for teaching expository craft presented in this book are based on the principles and practices of CraftPlus, a writing instruction program developed by Marcia S. Freeman. If you are familiar with CraftPlus, you will have an understanding of terms used in this book, such as *Target Skills®*, *models*, and *genre blocks*. If you are not familiar with CraftPlus, a "Quick Review of CraftPlus" is provided in Appendix A (see page 84).

This book will directly address expository writing that *informs* or *explains how*. There will not be as much information about writing that *explains why*, as persuasive writing is covered in depth in another book in this series.

> Who Teaches How to Write an Expository Paper?

Students begin to develop the building blocks of good expository writing in kindergarten. Sorting and classifying are imperative to learning how to organize an expository paper. Creating lists of related items, identifying descriptive attributes, and collecting data prepares students for providing the supporting details needed for effective expository writing.

As students mature into emergent writers they should begin writing personal exposition: *This is my cat. Her name is Ginger. She is a Manx cat and she weighs 26 pounds. I think my cat is very special.* In second and third grades, students begin learning to add transitions that create continuity and smooth flow in their writing. They begin to analyze and compare traits and to use comparative language.

By the time they reach fourth grade students are ready for explicit, concentrated instruction in expository craft. From fourth to tenth grades, students should receive direct instruction to develop fluency, quality of supporting details, and engaging style in all types of expository writing.

By adopting a progressive writing curriculum (such as CraftPlus®), schools can ensure uniformity of curriculum, and teachers at any grade level can rely on prerequisite skills being taught.

> The Instructional Sequence

Here is the instructional sequence for teaching expository craft:

- Step One: Developing Details
- Step Two: Creating Organization
- Step Three: Writing an Expository Paragraph
- Step Four: Writing an Expository Paper
- Step Five: Revising and Editing

These five steps are covered in Chapters Two through Six of this book. Each chapter includes a detailed description of why, how, and when to teach the step, complete with lesson plans, modifications, examples, assessment ideas, and an instructional timeline. Lessons are designed to be taught consecutively, and most of the writing that students produce will be considered practice. Periodic assessment is built into each step.

There are thirty-two lessons presented in this book. Taught consecutively, the specific skills essential to well-crafted expository writing could be taught well within the time frame of a nine-week period, or could be modified to fit into a single six-week term.

> Writers' Notebooks

Before you begin to teach these writing lessons, be sure that each of your students has a writers' notebook. I recommend loose-leaf binders so that students can take pages in and out, add paper when needed, and use tabs to divide the notebook into sections. These notebooks will be very important for having students store their work, ideas, and reference materials.

You may modify tabbed sections in the Writers' Notebooks to meet your needs, but suggested sections for each student notebook are

- Writing Practice—a section for the Target Skill practice work students complete during workshop time
- Resources—a place for students to store printed reference materials and writing-craft examples
- Editing/Revising—a place to keep editing and revising checklists and resources
- Works in Progress—a place to keep individual writing ideas and projects
- Published Work—a place to keep finished pieces

> Lessons

Lessons presented in this book are designed for students in grades four through ten. You should always feel free to modify the lessons to fit the developmental stages and needs of your students. Modifications and suggestions for alternative strategies are also supplied throughout the text. Some student samples are provided in Appendix C (see page 103). These samples are derived from students at various levels of this age range and various degrees of proficiency.

Lesson plans are structured to fit a 30-45 minute block of time. Each lesson follows the sequence of mini-lesson, workshop, and response. For introductory lessons, the mini-lesson portion always outweighs the workshop and response time. As students become more proficient with Target Skills, the teacher-directed time should decrease and the workshop time should increase.

For example, an introductory lesson might look like this:

- **Mini-Lesson (15 minutes):** Introduce and define skill. Provide examples and models. Allow students opportunities to generate new examples and models.
- **Workshop (15 minutes):** At the introductory level, students might work in pairs or cooperative groups to generate new examples and ideas. The teacher should circulate, monitor, and assist students as needed. (As students become more fluent with the skills, they should work individually.)
- **Response (10-15 minutes):** During this time, students will share their work with other members of the class, either in pairs, small groups, or in an author's chair setting. The teacher and student peers should comment upon the examples, affirm the students' understanding of the skill, and articulate the qualities inherent in the examples.

In busy classrooms with limited instructional periods, it is not realistic to assume you can maintain this lesson structure on a daily basis. Feel free to tailor the scheduling: the approximately 15-minute mini-lesson portion can be taught as a small portion of your instructional time, and the follow-up workshop and response can be completed in another setting or class period. Suggestions for such segmenting of the lesson structures are listed in the modifications that follow each lesson plan.

> Models

Throughout this book, you will be advised to use literary models to provide students with examples of Target Skills as used by professional writers. This modeling is essential for giving your students a clear picture of the goal they will seek to achieve in their own writing. One of the CraftPlus core resources, *Models for Teaching Writing-Craft Target Skills* (see Bibliography on page 83), provides lists of published works that you can use for literature models. Be sure to locate and assemble models ahead of time so that they are easily accessible when you are teaching each lesson.

As lessons continue and your students accumulate practice, their pieces should also serve as positive models. Models from your own classroom are inherently meaningful to your students. You should copy and save student models to use in subsequent years. Appendix C (see page 103) provides some student models that you may use as well.

> Assessment

Within each chapter detailing an instructional step, you will find suggestions for assessing your students. While most of their writing will be considered practice, you will periodically assess their proficiency with the skills you are teaching. Feel free to use the included assessment rubrics and weighted checklists as they are, or alter them as needed to fit the assessment requirements of your school or district.

> Remember

You know your students. Adjust the length of each lesson or the rate of the instructional sequence to fit their developmental levels and needs. You know your curriculum as well. Adjust the presentation of these skills to integrate subject areas as you are able. Similarly, you know your school's environment. You may wish to work with a peer or a teaching team to gain collegial support in sharing ideas and gathering materials.

In the end, this book will provide the map and provisions, but the journey is yours.

CHAPTER TWO

Step One—Details

> The Primary Importance of Details

Details are the most important element of expository writing: An attorney builds a case by collecting evidence. A doctor reaches a diagnosis by examining symptoms. A chef creates a gourmet delicacy by assembling ingredients. In the same way, writers communicate their message with details. Every detail is another piece of evidence that supports the thesis statement.

I say that details are of "primary" importance because they should be the starting point for good expository writing. Often, teachers stress organization over content. This approach requires students to create an organizational template and then fill it in with the details. While most of us can admit that we have required students to create a thesis statement and three main sub-topics *prior* to developing the supporting details, hopefully we can all learn to abandon this approach.

I discovered the need for beginning with the supporting details when I took a district-wide expository writing assessment alongside my students. I read the prompt and immediately began drawing the organizational template on my planning sheet. After all, that was what I had taught my students to do. But after I drew three boxes, I came to a halt. I realized I didn't know how to organize the body of my paper since I didn't know which details I would include.

I was stuck. The prompt required the young writers to explain how they would change their daily schedule if given the opportunity. I quickly discovered that the first thing I needed to do was make a list of everything I did during a typical day. I needed to look at those *details* before I could decide what changes I would make.

After making a list of details, I realized I had a format decision to make. I could structure the body of my piece with three paragraphs, focusing on my morning, midday, and evening routines, or I could form two paragraphs, focusing on the things I would change and the things I would leave the same. It was liberating to know that I had a choice.

When I discussed my experience with my students, I learned something interesting. Four students enthusiastically spoke up and said they had experienced the same epiphany at some point in the past, and always began by listing details. It came as no surprise that these students were some of my best writers.

While proficient writers might discover the need to begin with details on their own, most students need to be taught to do so. Teach students to begin planning for expository writing by making a list of details. An organizational structure will emerge from that list, and meaningful, well-supported writing will be the end product.

> Listing

Most people are natural list-makers. We make grocery lists, "to do" lists, lists of baby and pet names. We sort our world into alphabetical phone listings, batting orders, movie schedules, agendas, and scientific classifications. For young writers, listing is an important way to build a concept from the ground up.

Details on a list provide a concrete framework for creating structure. By asking young students to create their main ideas first, we put them in the position of having to pull ideas from thin air. Teaching students to begin prewriting by making lists of details allows them to sort and categorize concrete elements into an organizational structure and develop their main ideas from tangible data.

The very youngest students do not need to attach written language to their lists. "Fist lists" are quick, easy ways to practice categorizing related items and are great fillers for brief periods of transition. Primary teachers can hold up a fist and say, *Tell me five words that begin with the /k/ sound; Let's list five animals that live in the understory of the rainforest; List five things you might see at the beach.* Fist lists take no equipment. The teacher begins with a fist in the air and raises one finger as each detail is listed.

When students are ready to apply written language to lists, you can write their details on chart paper. One practical listing activity is the ABC list. Write the alphabet vertically down a sheet of long chart paper, from A to Z. Give students a concept and have them generate at least one item for each letter of the alphabet. These lists are great continuous collections of concepts or objects studied during a content-area unit.

When reviewing material in any content area, lists of "What We Know about ________" provide students with a concrete review of facts and concepts. Encourage students to supply the details they remember about a topic of study and write them on chart paper. In this way, you prepare them for creating lists of details while informally assessing their learning.

When you're ready to foster independent list-making, you can give students a topic and have them generate individual lists. Lists can be developed in class or as homework. Bring everyone together after this assignment to compare lists and provide peer modeling.

Lists can be categorized according to descriptive attributes. You can list physical attributes, character traits, properties, etc. You can have a child describe a place by asking for sensory impressions: *What do you see, smell, hear, taste, feel?* Listing descriptive attributes not only helps prepare students for writing with a wealth of supporting details, it also helps them build the vocabulary of good writers.

If students have practiced listing related details in these and other ways, they are well prepared to generate lists of details in response to a prompt. They are also prepared to use their lists to create an organizational structure for writing.

> Types of Details

Once students have a handle on creating lists of supporting details, it is important to teach them about the various types of details they can employ. Variety will add quality to their writing craft and will provide a broad base of support for a thesis statement or main idea.

There are several main categories under which most details can be categorized. Each can serve a different purpose. Numbers and statistics add credibility to support by making it measurable. Brief narratives give a personal quality to the support and invite the reader to connect to the text. Direct quotes substantiate support by adding a source outside the author and reader.

While writers can purposely choose the types of details they use as support, young writers should be taught to consciously apply a varied arsenal of support. Teach them not to overuse any one type of detail.

Most supporting details will fall into these categories:

- Facts
- Self-Evident Truths
- Anecdotes (narrative vignettes)
- Comparison or analogies
- Authoritative quotes or testimonials
- Numbers/Statistics
- Descriptive Details
- Definition
- Graphics (diagrams, maps, charts, bulleted lists, etc.)

The best way I have found to teach students to write various types of details is to first lead them to discover these types of details in published works. Expository articles in magazines, non-fiction trade books, newspaper articles and content-area textbooks are all fertile grounds for hunting details. If students "discover" and classify different types of details on their own, you can assist them in applying names to the types of details. Once the types of details have names, your class will have a shared working vocabulary for writing conferences and suggested revisions.

> Description

Writing that contains clear, specific, descriptive attributes is both engaging and credible. Attributes can be **concrete** (*color, height, temperature, shape, texture, etc.*) or **abstract** (*durability, stability, quality, agility, etc.*). Younger students should stick to the concrete end of the continuum, as abstract attributes require more maturity and discernment. As writers mature, they should be taught to employ both concrete and abstract descriptive attributes.

Descriptive attributes could consume an entire teaching unit and be applied across every genre. For our purposes, we will devote two lessons to the development of descriptive attributes for use in expository writing. Optional Lesson Ideas (see page 22) address this topic if you would like to devote more time and attention than allotted in the basic sequence of lessons.

Descriptive attributes should be specific. Students need to develop vocabulary that will allow for precise word choices, and they should maintain dynamic vocabulary lists in their writers' notebooks. Teach your students that they can avoid general statements by planning for both concrete and abstract attributes and by employing a Target Skill called "Don't Hit Your Reader over the Head."

"Don't Hit Your Reader over the Head" refers to writing that allows for inferential reading. Rather than hitting the reader over the head by making a general statement like, "He looked sad," the writer uses precise language to describe the gait, posture, and facial expressions that lead the reader to conclude that the character looks sad.

Teaching your young writers to use specific descriptive attributes will instantly improve the quality of their support. As readers, they will see the value in being able to visualize details and interact with the text. They will want their own writing to be as clear and accessible. Additionally, they will be developing a skill that they will be able to apply to any genre of writing.

> Getting Ready

Plan for a 10-15 minute mini-lesson, a 15-20 minute writing workshop, and about 10 minutes of response time for each lesson. You can teach each lesson in one forty-five minute class period, or you can divide lessons into sections as needed (see modifications that follow each lesson).

Gather materials for each lesson. Some examples and literature models are provided in the lessons. However, you can easily substitute your own. Use models and examples that are meaningful to your students and appropriate to their stage of writing development.

Many teachers find it helpful to develop an instructional writing notebook. This is a place to store your lesson plans, student samples, resources, and reproducibles so that they are at your fingertips when you present the lessons from class to class and from year to year.

> Stages of Writing Development

CraftPlus writing levels are defined as:

- **Initial (approximately K-1 grade students)**—Initial writers are developing the speech-to-print connection. Writers begin to write related sentences, but sentences are simple and repetitive in structure.
- **Developing (approximately 2-3 grade students)**—Developing writers are becoming comfortable with writing connected text. They begin to vary sentence structure and write in paragraph format.
- **Fluent (approximately 4-5 grade students)**—Fluent writers are capable of multi-paragraphed pieces, writing for multiple genres, and applying composing skills.
- **Fluent Plus (generally middle-school age)**—Fluent Plus writers use literary devices, composing skills, precise words choices, and clear organizational formats to create pieces that flow logically across many genres.

Most of the lessons in this book are aimed at writers in the Fluent and Fluent Plus stages of writing development. However, simple modifications can tailor the lessons to meet the needs of writers who have not reached these levels.

> Points to Remember

Teach students to begin planning for expository writing with *details*. Organization and structure will follow this important first step. Be sure to model processes and allow students to participate in modeling. They need to try each skill out orally before trying it in writing. Feel free to modify your lessons to meet the needs and levels of your students. Be sure that students can generate strong, varied details before moving to Step Two—Organization.

> The Lessons

The lessons in Step One will prepare students for generating a wealth of details as a starting point for expository writing. This step is designed to be taught in a sequence of six lessons. For each lesson, modifications are provided to accommodate varying levels of student abilities or time constraints. Optional Lesson Ideas (see page 22) to reinforce the skills being taught can be found at the end of the chapter.

Lesson 1: Listing Details	Materials: Literature models, writers' notebooks	Objective: Students will work cooperatively to create a list of details for a given topic.
Lesson 2: Types of Supporting Details	Materials: Newspapers, "how-to" books or content-area textbooks, writers' notebooks	Objective: Students will identify specific types of supporting details in text.
Lesson 3: Developing Descriptive Attributes	Materials: Two picture prompts or unusual objects to display, writers' notebooks	Objective: Students will work cooperatively to create a web of descriptive attributes.
Lesson 4: Writing with Descriptive Attributes	Materials: Picture prompts, writers' notebooks	Objective: Students will work cooperatively to plan and write descriptions of a given picture.
Lesson 5: Don't Hit Your Reader over the Head	Materials: Copy of *"Don't Hit Your Reader over the Head" Activity Cards* (see page 98), writers' notebooks	Objective: Students will work in pairs to create a description that allows for inferential reading.
Lesson 6: Assessment	Materials: Expository prompt, rubric	Objective: Students will create a list of at least 10 details for a given prompt and identify descriptive attributes for three of those details.

Lesson 1: Listing Details

Objective: Students will work cooperatively to create a list of details for a given topic.

Materials: Literature models, writers' notebooks

Mini-Lesson (15-20 minutes)

Introduce the concept that expository writing has an inherent purpose to inform, explain why, or tell how. Explain to students that for each purpose, supporting details provide the weight of the piece. Good vocabulary, focus, organization, and conventions are important, but without compelling supporting details the piece is empty. Offer a non-example, such as:

> Abraham Lincoln was mostly self-educated. He taught himself to read and was perpetually seeking reading material. He read many of his favorite books more than once. He grew to have an affection for poetry and could spontaneously recite many famous poems. His cousin reported seeing young Abe with a book in his pocket at all times, ready to read whenever there was a break in the grueling farm work to which he was born.

This paragraph remains focused, contains a variety of sentence structures, and can even boast of some strong vocabulary. However, this paragraph is lacking in specific details the reader can visualize. Offer an example of a paragraph that is well-supported, like this one from *Lincoln: A Photobiography*, by Russell Freedman.

> Mostly, he educated himself by borrowing books and newspapers. There are many stories about Lincoln's efforts to find enough books to satisfy him in that backwoods country. Those he liked he read again and again, losing himself in the adventures of *Robison Crusoe* or the magical tales of *The Arabian Nights*. He was thrilled by a biography of George Washington, with its stirring account of the Revolutionary War. And he came to love the rhyme and rhythm of poetry, reciting passages from Shakespeare or the Scottish poet Robert Burns at the drop of a hat. He would carry a book out to the field with him, so he could read at the end of each plow furrow, while the horse was getting its breath. When noon came, he would sit under a tree and read while he ate. "I never saw Abe after he was twelve that he didn't have a book in his hand or in his pocket," Dennis Hanks remembered. "It didn't seem natural to see a feller read like that."

This paragraph contains all of the elements of the first, but it is packed with a greater number of specific, well-crafted supporting details. Ask students to compare the quality of each paragraph and lead them in a discussion of the differences between the two. Once they form a concept of the value of supporting details, they are ready to learn to plan for using them.

Explain to students that well-supported writing begins with the details. A thesis statement, sub-topics, and an organizational structure will emerge from an abundant list of details. Lead students in brainstorming a list of details about a subject familiar to all of them (e.g., your school environment, the importance of libraries, information about telephones, a current event, or current topic of study). Write details on the board as students provide them. Gather at least twenty details about the given topic. Ask students, *Would we be able to create a well-supported piece of writing using these details?*

Workshop (5-10 minutes)

Arrange the class in small groups of three or four students. Give each group a piece of paper and assign the same topic to all groups. For example, if you teach a content area and have been studying a certain topic, use that topic as an integrated review. Otherwise, choose a topic familiar to all (e.g., dress code, weather, food, media). Ask each group to generate a list of as many details as possible related to this topic. Establish a time limit for accomplishing this task and set a timer (probably about five minutes).

Response (5-10 minutes)

When time is up, ask one group read their list. Each subsequent group should read only the details on their lists not already read by another group. Affirm responses and refine students' understanding of related details by pointing out details that are not directly related to the topic. Students can defend their choices to articulate their thinking if they feel so led. End the lesson by reminding students that whether they are being asked to inform, explain why, or tell how, all expository writing is best supported when the writer begins with the details.

Modifications

- Each group can be given a different topic. This may work best with older students. Specify for these groups whether their purpose is to inform, explain why, or tell how. This will narrow the focus of the details listed.
- Assign pairs instead of small groups. This allows you the opportunity to informally assess student engagement and understanding.
- If time is limited, the first portion of the lesson could be presented in one day, with workshop and response presented on the following day.
- If time is limited, the workshop activity can be assigned on an individual basis as homework, and response can take the form of a review at the beginning of the next lesson.
- If topics are related to content-area studies and you wish to create a truly integrated lesson, provide resources from which details can be derived and lengthen the time allotted for the detail hunt.
- You can provide a template for students if you feel they would benefit from a structural format. Students can be asked to create an ABC list or can be given categories of details to list (e.g., sensory, physical, abstract).

No matter what modifications you may choose to employ, do not skip the essential step of modeling the process of listing details during the mini-lesson. The structure of the practice can be altered, but the opportunity to practice must not be skipped. Generally, the younger the students, the more general the topic should be. Older students can handle more specific topics.

Lesson 2: Types of Supporting Details

Objective: Identify specific types of details in text.

Materials: Literature model, newspapers, "how-to" books or content-area texts, writers' notebooks

Mini-Lesson (15-20 minutes)

At the beginning of this lesson, briefly review your main objectives from the previous lesson (details create well-supported writing, and planning should begin with the supporting details). Reread the well-supported paragraph from the previous lesson, whether it was one of your own choosing or the example provided in the text.

> **1.** Mostly, he educated himself by borrowing books and newspapers. **2.** There are many stories about Lincoln's efforts to find enough books to satisfy him in that backwoods country. **3.** Those he liked he read again and again, losing himself in the adventures of *Robison Crusoe* or the magical tales of *The Arabian Nights.* **4.** He was thrilled by a biography of George Washington, with its stirring account of the Revolutionary War. **5.** And he came to love the rhyme and rhythm of poetry, reciting passages from Shakespeare or the Scottish poet Robert Burns at the drop of a hat. **6.** He would carry a book out to the field with him, so he could read at the end of each plow furrow, while the horse was getting its breath. **7.** When noon came, he would sit under a tree and read while he ate. **8.** "I never saw Abe after he was twelve that he didn't have a book in his hand or in his pocket," Dennis Hanks remembered. **9.** "It didn't seem natural to see a feller read like that."

After reading the selection, explain to students that details fall into several discrete categories. Ask students to identify the supporting details, one at a time. As they identify the individual details, discuss the type of information provided in each detail.

For example, sentence #1 has two concrete examples embedded in the main idea statement. Sentence #2 is a general example, using the word "many" but not citing specific stories. Sentences #3, #4, and #5 provide specific, concrete examples that give the reader a sense of the breadth of Lincoln's literary interests. Sentences #6 and #7 provide a narrative vignette, or anecdote. The paragraph ends with an authoritative quote from Lincoln's cousin in sentences #8 and #9.

Begin listing the types of details you find on the board. You may use the list provided, or work with students to rename each category in a way that is meaningful to your class. Types of details generally fall into these categories:

- Specific or Concrete Examples
- Facts
- Self-Evident Truths
- Anecdotes (narrative vignettes)
- Comparison or analogies
- Authoritative quotes or testimonials
- Numbers/Statistics
- Descriptive Details
- Definition
- Graphics (diagrams, maps, charts, bulleted lists, etc.)

After creating the list, post it in the classroom for future reference. Students should copy the list and store it in the resource section of their writers' notebooks. If you use the language provided above, you can copy *Types of Supporting Details with Examples* (see page 88) from the reproducible section of this book.

Workshop (15 minutes)

During workshop, students will conduct a detail hunt. Newspapers, "how-to" books, and content-area textbooks are very potent texts for this activity. Arrange the class in pairs of students. Over the course of ten minutes, each pair is to read an article, chapter, or chapter sub-section. As they read, they should make a list of the types of details they find. Set a timer so that students will begin and end promptly. Circulate and assist as students conduct their searches. At the end of ten minutes, students will stop the search and prepare for response time.

Response (5-10 minutes)

Ask each pair to report the types of details they located and to provide examples. If time permits, have each pair report. If time is limited, name a type of detail from the list and ask students to provide an example of that type of detail from their texts.

Modifications

- With younger students, you will want to identify the text they will be searching. For example, give each pair a specific newspaper article or chapter sub-section. More mature students will benefit from finding their own article or selection.
- If you use a newspaper, students can highlight the details for easy reference at response time.
- If you feel the need to provide greater support and structure, prepare a practice exercise with articles contrived to meet the needs of the assignment.
- If time is limited, this lesson can be divided into two days, with the mini-lesson presented on the first day and the workshop/response times presented on the second day.
- Students can perform the workshop activity independently for homework, with extended response time provided at the beginning of the next lesson to be sure each student has a firm understanding of the various types of details.

No matter what modifications you may choose to employ, be sure to model the detail hunt before assigning it to students and provide adequate response time to clarify any misconceptions.

Lesson 3: Developing Descriptive Attributes

Objective: Developing descriptive attributes.

Materials: Picture prompts or unusual objects to display for class (one for modeling, one for student workshop), writers' notebooks.

Mini-Lesson (15-20 minutes)

Explain to students that descriptive specificity allows the reader to visualize or otherwise vicariously experience a piece of writing. Read from a literature model that contains specific descriptive attributes. See *Models for Teaching Writing-Craft Target Skills* or use science-themed magazines written for young readers.

Be sure your literature model contains many examples of specific descriptive attributes. Read the article or excerpt in its entirety first, and then review the piece slowly, stopping at each descriptive attribute. Point out the first few descriptive attributes, and then allow students to identify others.

Display a picture or object so that the whole class can see it. Animal photos, ornamental decorative items, and unusual plants make good focal points. Use a concept web (see page 91) to model for students the development of descriptive attributes. Consciously group attributes into categories, but do not tell students the categories.

For example:

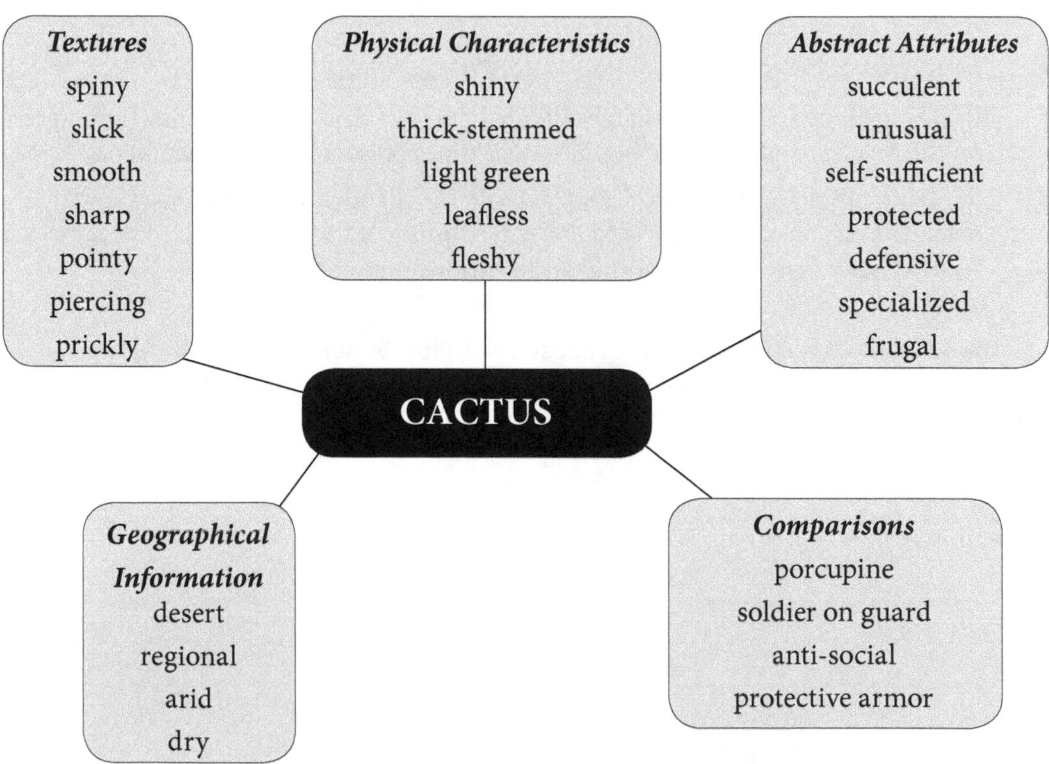

Lead students to discover categories as you think out loud and form your descriptive attribute concept web. Invite students to provide more descriptive attributes to add to your web.

Workshop (10 minutes)

Display a picture or unusual object so all students can easily see it. Arrange students in groups of three. Each group will create a descriptive attribute concept web like the one modeled during the mini-lesson. Webs should contain at least four categories of descriptive attributes.

Response (5-10 minutes)

Each group will share their concept web. You may want to create a collective web as they share, listing all descriptive attributes and building categories. This collective web can be displayed in the classroom alongside the picture or object that is described in the web.

Modifications

- If you want to collect many different webs to display in the classroom, you can give each group a separate picture. The pictures can be attached to the webs for display.
- If time is limited, you can present the mini-lesson one day and workshop/response the next day.
- If time is limited, students can select or be assigned pictures cut from magazines and create attribute webs as a homework assignment. However, if time allows for workshop activity in class, students will benefit from conversation and shared ideas.
- Direct students to select pictures from a collection and create descriptive attribute webs. After sharing a web, other students can guess the identity of the object in the picture.

Lesson 4: Writing with Descriptive Attributes

Objective: Write descriptions of picture prompts using a variety of descriptive attributes.

Materials: Web modeled in previous lesson, picture prompts, writers' notebooks

Mini-Lesson (15 minutes)

Use the web from the previous lesson to model the development of well-written descriptive sentences. Think out loud to demonstrate at first. Then invite students to offer descriptive sentences generated from the attributes in the web.

Developing example: *The cactus is leafless, pointy, and sharp. It is protected by its prickly, unusual flesh. The cactus is like a porcupine in the desert.*

Fluent example: *Spiny, piercing thorns protect the leafless stems. This porcupine of the desert is protected by its prickly armor.*

Fluent Plus example: *Fleshy, thick, leafless stems sit attentively, like a soldier on guard. Spiny thorns protect this horticultural porcupine.*

Workshop (15-20 minutes)

Arrange students in groups of three or four. Distribute picture prompts to each group. Students will work cooperatively to develop an attribute web and write at least three descriptive sentences using the attributes in the web.

Response (10 minutes)

A spokesperson from each group will share the group's web and descriptive sentences. Provide positive feedback related to the target (specificity, variety of descriptive attributes).

Modifications

- Rather than providing picture prompts, students can be asked in advance to bring in pictures for this workshop activity.
- If time is limited, this lesson can be broken into two sessions. I would not advise assigning this workshop as homework, because the collaborative effort will support students in bridging from attribute lists to descriptive writing.
- If students need more support, continue a full descriptive writing about the web created in the previous lesson. Focus on allowing students to create descriptive sentences from the web. The picture-prompted group writing can be done in a subsequent lesson.
- If students need more support, repeat the web model with the class using a different object or picture. Increase the students' level of interaction this time.
- If you determine that your students need additional practice, assign a similar activity for homework or independent workshop before moving on to the next lesson.

Lesson 5: Don't Hit Your Reader over the Head

Objective: Write for inferential reading using the Target Skill "Don't Hit Your Reader over the Head."

Materials: Literature model(s), *"Don't Hit Your Reader over the Head"* Activity Cards (see page 98) cut into individual cards.

Mini-Lesson (15-20 minutes)

Explain to students that readers enjoy books that allow them to think as they read, become involved in the story, make predictions and interact with the text. Writers have the responsibility of creating text that allows the reader to think. Tell your students that one way to do this is to avoid making general statements that "hit the reader over the head." Instead, the writer should build clues and offer specific details that allow the reader to arrive at a conclusion without being directly told. Offer a literature model, such as this paragraph from Gary Paulsen's *Father Water, Mother Woods: Essays on Fishing and Hunting in the North Woods*:

> Grades bad, clothes wrong, never any money, hair that never worked into a flattop or a ducktail—just impossible. To wear wrong clothes and be from the wrong place in town and have the wrong parents and think the wrong thoughts and to feel, to suspect, to know that everyone is looking, pointing, laughing. School.

Lead a discussion about how this persona feels about school. Point out that the author could have just written, "I didn't like school and I felt like I didn't fit in." Talk about how this would have stated his feelings, but in a much less interesting, less compelling way.

Give students this statement: *He loved school and excelled in every subject.* Ask students to offer details that will build clues so that a reader could figure the statement out without being told it directly. Write their ideas on the board and form your own class example of *"Don't Hit Your Reader over the Head."*

Workshop (10 minutes)

Arrange class into pairs. (In preparation for this activity, you should have copied the "Don't Hit Your Reader over the Head" Activity Cards and cut them into individual cards.) You will give each pair of students a direct-statement activity card and they will work together to develop descriptive details that allow the reader to infer the information that is not directly stated.

Response (15 minutes)

Each pair will read their description to the class without divulging the sentence on their activity card. After each piece is read, allow other students an opportunity to identify the original direct statement based on the clues provided.

Modifications

- If time is limited, you can assign one direct statement to each student for homework and begin the next lesson with response.
- If time is limited, you can divide the lesson with the mini-lesson portion on the first day and the workshop/response time on the second day.
- Students may want to write their own direct statements rather than using the prepared statements that you supply. They can submit statements to you for your approval and you can distribute them for the workshop activity.
- If students have difficulty with the concept, be sure to read other literature models in addition to the one provided. You may want to model more than one example during the mini-lesson as well.
- Ask students to hunt for examples and non-examples of "Don't Hit Your Reader over the Head" in expository texts such as textbooks and newspaper articles.

Lesson 6: Assessment

Objective: Assessment.

Materials: Loose-leaf paper for assessment, rubric or scoring method, expository prompt

Mini-Lesson (5-10 minutes)

Conduct a brief review by asking students to tell what they have learned about details during these lessons. Be sure that students understand the importance of planning details as an initial step to writing an expository piece. Review types of supporting details, descriptive attributes, and writing for inferential reading. Allow students to assist you in creating a varied detail list for an expository prompt. List a minimum of ten basic details. Select three or four details for which you will list descriptive attributes.

Example: *Write to tell how to take care of a dog.*

- *Food*
- *Bed—washable, durable fabric, aesthetic value, soft padding*
- *Walks*
- *Vaccinations*
- *Vet—convenient location, accessible hours, certified, recommendations, cost*
- *Grooming*
- *Collar—size-appropriate, width, choker vs. buckled, complementary color,*
- *License*
- *Toys*
- *Medications*
- *Training—books, videos, rewards, consistency, obedience school*
- *Leash*

Assessment

Provide students with a general expository prompt (see page 97). Each student will create a list of at least ten specific details directly related to the prompt. For at least three of the details, they will write descriptive attributes.

Scoring

For this assessment, you may use either a rubric or weighted checklist. Rubrics are well suited to evaluating students' developing level of competency toward mastery of specific Target Skills. However, if you are in a situation where you must derive a percentage for each student's score, a weighted checklist is ideal. Examples of both a rubric and a weighted checklist for this assessment are provided on page 23. Additional assessment rubrics for both single and multiple Target Skills can be found on pages 99 and 100.

I have found it best to provide a minimum passing score, which in most schools is 60%, for completing the assignment. For the other criteria, you can assign a portion of the points as needed (e.g., 6 out of 10 points if only 6 details are listed).

> Optional Lesson Ideas

- Letter Writing—Students can write to pen pals or relatives telling about your school or class.
- Integrated Detail Lists—If you teach other content areas, create lists of main ideas and details for textbook selections. These can be done as a whole group, small group, or individual format.
- Expert Lists—Have each student select a topic on which they are, or want to be, an expert. Each student should state the topic and gather as many details as possible about the topic.
- Sensory Field Trips—Take a walk to an outdoor location on your campus. Have students list sensory details (sights, sounds, smells, textures, etc.).
- Field Trip Detail Lists—After a field trip, create lists of details about the trip. This can be done as a whole group, small group, or individual format.
- Create Visuals—Create graphs, charts, webs, and other visual aids using details.
- Process Lists—The lessons in Step One predominantly address details associated with "explain why" or "give information about" prompts. We will discuss planning for "how-to" pieces in the next chapter. However, you can provide practice for students in listing steps to processes (e.g., how to make a milkshake, how to study for a test, how to catch a fish).

Sample Rubric for Details and Descriptive Attributes

Name:____ **Date:**__________________________

Target Skills: Details with Descriptive Attributes

Directions: List at least ten details related to the prompt. Write descriptive attributes for at least three of the details.	**Score**
Applies Target Skills competently and creatively	3
Applies Target Skills competently	2
Attempts to apply Target Skills	1
Makes no attempt to apply Target Skills	Not scoreable

Sample Weighted Checklist for Details and Descriptive Attributes

Name:____ **Date:**______________________

Target Skills: Details and Descriptive Attributes

Student Initials	**Criteria**	**Points Available**	**Points Achieved**
	Assignment is complete	60	
	Ten details related to the prompt	10	
	Descriptive attributes for detail	10	
	Descriptive attributes for detail	10	
	Descriptive attributes for detail	10	

CHAPTER THREE
Step Two—Organization

> Organization from Details

Once you feel confident that students understand the importance of details and can construct thorough lists of varied details and descriptive attributes, teach them to organize from those details. Organization obviously involves structure, which can be built from detail lists through the use of careful planning and graphic organizers. Organization also involves the relationship between ideas in the piece that provides a logical progression and develops a central theme or focus.

There are various graphic organizers addressed in this chapter. Through using them, students will learn to clump details together into groups of related information, establish a rationale for each group, sequence groups of information, and develop a focus. (The exception to this organizational process is the "how-to" paper, which shows the steps in a process. Rather than clumps of related details, these papers will be structured in chronological order.)

Explain to students that most of the expository prompts that they will encounter will be written in present tense, and that most expository writing should be written in present tense as well. Even if a prompt is written in future tense, present tense is the best choice for the response. The exception to this rule is a prompt that addresses a historical event, such as: *Discuss possible explanations for the disappearance of the Roanoke Colony.* A response to such a prompt would necessarily be written in past tense.

> The Structure of Expository Writing

The traditional structure of most expository writing is the classic three-point, five-paragraph paper. Many schools and districts have finally rejected this format as being formulaic and stale. However, sometimes students are still required to write in this formulaic structure, so it is important to be sure they know how to organize and construct this type of paper.

Once your students understand the traditional structure, teach them to apply their own creativity and style within an organizational framework. Teach the function of each paragraph within the expository paper: The introductory paragraph hooks the reader and presents the topic or thesis. Each body paragraph presents a sub-topic and supporting details. The closing paragraph brings the supported focus to a logical conclusion.

Within the body of the paper, students will apply organizational writing-craft skills, such as topic sentences and transitional phrases. If your school has been using CraftPlus as a comprehensive writing curriculum, you can focus on the application of these skills. If your students do not have a background with these Target Skills, you may need to extend the lessons so that students are working at a mastery level.

> Instructional Level

Within the CraftPlus curriculum, Target Skills spiral in difficulty over succeeding years. Many skills repeat from year to year, with an increased level of instruction and student expectations. With all Target Skills, there are three main levels of students' understanding and application:

- **A—Awareness**: Students know what the Target Skill is, can identify it in literature models, may use it orally, and might use it in writing during shared and interactive writing experiences, or through revision with a teacher's guidance.
- **I—Instructional**: Students practice using the skill orally and in writing, but may overgeneralize and might not use it effectively.
- **M—Mastery**: Students consistently, effectively, and independently use the Target Skill in their writing.

Generally, these instructional levels coordinate with student ages or grade levels. At the ages addressed by this book, students will experience the greatest success if they are working at a mastery level with general Target Skills so that they are focused on the expository genre and can apply the writing-craft skills they have mastered.

> Points to Remember

As students begin to use graphic organizers and arrange their details into related clumps of information, you must be sure they don't forget the primary importance of details discussed in the previous chapter. Well-supported expository writing begins with the details. Now that students have begun using graphic organizers, they might try to start with the template instead of the detail list. However, they must begin with the details.

Students were introduced to several different types of organizational templates. They should choose the type of graphic organizers that works best for them. However, if you notice that a student is not successful with the type of graphic organizer they chose, intervene and suggest another type.

At this point, students have worked on the prewriting stage of the writing process. Before moving to the next step, I would have students select a writing plan they have already created from their writers' notebooks and develop it into a written piece. This would give them a chance to apply the skills they have developed, practice writing connected text, and create a rough draft to keep in their writers' notebooks for future revision and editing practice.

> The Lessons

The lessons comprising this step build upon the details students have worked to develop. In some lessons, students will develop details and organize them into related clumps. In other lessons, they can draw upon the details generated during the previous series of lessons, which should be stored in the practice section of their writers' notebooks.

Graphic organizers are introduced and practiced in Lesson 2a. There are several organizational templates provided in this text. However, you may have graphic organizers of your own, and students may have templates they are comfortable using. The purpose of Lesson 2a is to show students that there are multiple ways to go about organizing their details.

In Lesson 2b, students will narrow their focus to select a graphic organizer. I always explain to students that every brain is unique, and that no graphic organizer is ideal for everyone. Encourage your students to take ownership of this choice and select the graphic organizer they feel is most appropriate for the prompt and for their own style of cognitive processing.

There are two types of organization addressed in this chapter:

- describing a process
- all other expository writing

Organization for describing a process is similar to the listing techniques used in the previous chapter, but with an established sequential order. All other expository writing involves clumping related details. After listing and clumping, students will learn to determine a focus for their pieces and apply organizational Target Skills such as beginning hooks, transitional phrases, and ending techniques.

Lesson 1: Clumping Details	Materials: Sticky notes, index cards, markers	Objective: Students will organize details into related groups.
Lesson 2a: Graphic Organizers	Materials: Graphic organizer templates (see pp. 89-92)	Objective: Students will be able to identify and use a variety of graphic organizers.
Lesson 2b: Selecting and Using a Graphic Organizer	Materials: Writers' notebooks	Objective: Students will be able to select and use an appropriate graphic organizer for a list of details.
Lesson 3: Determining Focus and Writing Topic Sentences	Materials: Content-area textbooks, non-fiction magazines and/or newspapers, graphic organizer from previous lesson, writers' notebooks	Objective: Students will use graphic organizers to determine the focus for an expository piece and will write topic sentences for paragraphs.
Lesson 4: Beginning Hooks	Materials: Literature models, *Beginning Hooks with Examples* (see page 94), writers' notebooks	Objective: Students will learn various techniques for writing an opening hook.
Lesson 5: Hunting for Transitional Phrases	Materials: Multiple age-appropriate magazines, non-fiction books and/or content-area textbooks	Objective: Students will generate lists of transitional phrases used in expository texts.
Lesson 6: Ending Techniques	Materials: Magazines and/or texts used in Lesson 4, writers' notebooks	Objective: Students will develop and practice techniques for composing conclusions.
Lesson 7: Organizing Steps to a Process	Materials: Process prompts, writers' notebooks	Objective: Students will list steps to a process in sequential order.
Lesson 8: Assessment	Materials: Writers' notebooks, process prompt, scoring rubric	Objective: Students will demonstrate mastery of using an organizational template and creating a list of steps to a process.

As in the previous chapter, modifications are suggested following each lesson, and ideas for optional lessons are listed at the end of the chapter (see page 39).

Lesson 1: Clumping Details

Objective: The students will organize details into related groups.

Materials: Sticky notes, index cards, markers

Mini-Lesson (15 minutes)

Conduct a whole-group discussion in which students generate details about a given topic. Recent shared experiences (such as a field trip) or a recent topic of comprehensive study are potent topics for this activity. **As students provide details, write them on sticky notes and stick them to the board. Do not attempt to create any order with the notes. Purposely place them in a very random assortment.** Once you feel you have exhausted the topic, or you have at least twenty to thirty details on the board, begin collectively seeking ways to physically clump details into categories (groups of related details). Ask students to link details together and provide a rationale (main idea) for their categories. Write the rationale above each group as it is formed. This physical linking creates a concrete representation of the mental processes students will need to master in order to organize their details effectively. The rationale gives them focus and direction.

Workshop (15-20 minutes)

Arrange students in groups of three or four. Provide each group with a stack of index cards. Give the class a new topic. Choose a topic that is either very general (e.g., communication, sports, housing, patriotism) or is meaningful to your students (e.g., a recent topic of study, a shared experience, a current issue at your school). The topic can be generated by the students with your help. Students are to work collectively to repeat the process you have modeled and practiced during the mini-lesson. They should record details on the index cards, physically sort the cards into related details, and provide a rationale for each group.

Response (5-10 minutes)

Encourage each group to share their related details and rationales. Since all groups will have the same topic, they will benefit from hearing the different assortment of details and rationales for sorting details into categories. Be sure to articulate and affirm each group's choices after they have shared.

Modifications

- If time is limited, conduct the mini-lesson one day and the workshop/response activity during a subsequent lesson.
- If students have difficulty sorting details into categories, you may need to provide extra support by repeating the sticky-note activity with a new topic, leading students into taking a bigger role by gradually decreasing your support.
- You may want to sort your sticky notes onto separate legal-sized papers, write the rationale on each paper, and save these for a writing activity when working on paragraph development.
- If you sense that students would benefit from independent practice, or if you want to assess your students' abilities to create categories and rationales, you can repeat the workshop activity as an independent activity with a new topic.
- Some students benefit from color-coding the groups as a further concrete physical sorting aid. Students can use highlighters to color-code related details.

Lesson 2a: Graphic Organizers

Objective: Students will learn to use a variety of graphic organizers.

Materials: One large copy of each graphic organizer found on pages 89-92, on chart paper or the board.

Mini-Lesson (15-20 minutes)

Post large replicas of the following graphic organizers on the board: the boxed flow chart, concept boxes, concept web, and outline. The concept boxes are similar to the sticky notes and index cards students used in the previous lesson. The flow chart is a similar concept, but arranges the clumps of related details in order and places the topic at the top and bottom of the chart. A concept web, which is probably very familiar to students, organizes clumps of related details without ordering them. Finally, the outline is a very traditional template and is well suited to linear thinkers.

Explain to students that there are many ways to organize details. However, while narrative writing is arranged in chronological order, most expository writing is organized in clumps of related details. (You may wish to mention that describing a process is the one exception to this convention.) Discuss how graphic organizers are a pictorial representation of the organization process.

Offer a general expository topic (but *not* a process prompt) and quickly list details on the board as students provide them. Briefly explain each graphic organizer. Select students to come to the board and sort the list into clumps of related details. These students should work simultaneously on the different organizational templates. Instruct them to call upon classmates for ideas and support. Guide students through this process. When the details have been sorted and placed on the various templates, review and articulate the way the information is organized in the various formats. Work with students to establish a rationale for each grouping of related details and write a short rationale (one to four words) for each. Save these graphic organizers for possible use in subsequent lessons.

Workshop (10-15 minutes)

Arrange students into four groups. Give each group a different graphic organizer. Provide a general expository prompt (but not a process prompt) to the class. Each group should work together to first list details and then organize them into clumps of related details on a graphic organizer. After organizing details, they should discuss and establish a rationale, or main idea, for each clump of related details.

Response (10 minutes)

A representative from each group should share their graphic organizer, articulating the group's process for clumping details and stating the main idea for each grouping. Be sure to positively reinforce the successful development and organization of details by each group.

Modifications

- If time is limited, complete the mini-lesson on one day and complete the workshop and response in a subsequent lesson.
- If students require more support, you can directly model use of each graphic organizer before having students attempt to use them.
- You may want to use lists of details from previous lessons to save time. You can use a list generated by the class during Step One, and students can use lists saved in their writers' notebooks rather than starting with a new prompt and listing details.
- If students have little or no experience using graphic organizers, you may need to break this lesson into four sessions, allowing the focus to be on one type of organizer at a time.
- Have students save these graphic organizers in their writers' notebooks for later lessons when they will be using them as a foundation for a written piece.
- Color-coding related items using a highlighter may provide additional support for students in sorting and classifying details in the list before they transfer them to the graphic organizer. They can highlight or put colored dots next to items on their detail lists before transferring the details to the graphic organizer.

Lesson 2b: Selecting and Using a Graphic Organizer

Objective: Students will be able to select an appropriate graphic organizer for a list of related details.

Materials: Writers' notebooks

Mini-Lesson (10 minutes)

Briefly review the four types of graphic organizers introduced in the previous lesson. Have samples posted in the classroom. Present a general expository prompt and have students create detail lists in their writers' notebooks. Stop them after about four minutes and review the details together. Discuss ways details might be organized on each of the organizational templates.

If students were successful with the previous lesson and can clump details into three groups, this is a good time to demonstrate how to sort details into two or four groups. A paper with three body paragraphs is traditional, but not magical.

Workshop (15-20 minutes)

Direct students to choose a graphic organizer, draw it in their writers' notebooks, and begin organizing their details onto the template. They should develop a rationale and write a brief main idea for each grouping. Students will work independently on this workshop activity.

Response (10-15 minutes)

Survey the class to find out how many students used each type of graphic organizer. Begin with one type of graphic organizer and ask students who used it to share their reasons for choosing this template, the rationale for each grouping, and some examples of details within each group. Continue this process with each type of organizer. Students need to save these assignments in their writers' notebooks for use during Lesson 3.

Modifications

- If time is limited, this lesson can become a homework assignment following Lesson 2a.
- If students need additional support before working independently with graphic organizers, allow them to work in pairs on this activity, and assign independent work as homework or as part of a subsequent lesson.
- You can provide copies of the graphic organizers rather than having students draw them. However, be sure to allow students to choose the type of graphic organizers they use.
- You can extend the response activity by grouping together students who used the same type of graphic organizer and allowing them to discuss their choices and their work before sharing with the entire class. This may help some students articulate the reasons for and benefits of their choices.
- You may want to save time by directing students to use detail lists from a previous lesson rather than having them generate new lists.
- Color-coding related items on the detail list using a highlighter may provide additional support for students in sorting and classifying details before they transfer them to the graphic organizer. Students can use markers to continue color-coding details as they fill in the graphic organizers.

Lesson 3: Determining Focus and Writing Topic Sentences

Objective: Students will use graphic organizers to determine the focus of an expository piece and will write topic sentences for paragraphs.

Materials: Literature models (textbooks, newspapers, and/or non-fiction magazines), writers' notebooks, graphic organizers from previous lesson

Mini-Lesson (15-20 minutes)

Lead your students in a discussion about main idea statements (topic sentences for each body paragraph). Use content-area textbooks, newspapers, or non-fiction magazines to determine focus (generally found in headings and titles) and search for main idea statements at the beginnings of paragraphs. Model the process of locating main idea statements and corresponding supporting details in the text, and then allow students to search independently for five minutes or less to locate one or two examples of main idea statements.

Ask students to share main idea statements they located, and to share a few of the supporting details provided in those paragraphs. Discuss focus (the overall concept the writer is trying to express to the reader). Display a graphic organizer completed during the mini-lesson portion of Lesson 2b. Discuss the rationale for each clump of related details. Model for students the formation of a main idea statement, or topic sentence, from this clump of related details. Ask students to help you turn the other rationales into complete sentences. After developing these main idea statements, collectively determine a focus for the piece. Write the focus at the top of the page. Stress to students that the overall focus is the message the writer is trying to transmit to the reader and that all details should support this message.

Workshop (10-15 minutes)

Direct students to locate the graphic organizers they created during Lesson 2b in their writers' notebooks. Students should work to create main idea statements for each clump of related details on their templates. Then, students should determine an overall focus for each piece.

Response (10 minutes)

Arrange students in pairs. Students should read their details and main idea statements to their partners, and then state the focus of the piece. When listening, students should first connect to the details (e.g., *I had those exact same details in my graphic organizer, but I didn't put them all together.*) Then, listeners should comment about the clarity of the main idea statements and focus, or offer a suggestion for improvement. Students should switch roles as listener and reader and then repeat the process. After peer conferencing, review the concept of main idea statements with the whole class and answer any questions students may have.

Modifications

- If peer conferencing is new to students, you should model the process by conducting a peer conference between the teacher and a student in front of the class before allowing students to conduct peer conferences.
- If time is limited, you can present the mini-lesson during class, assign the workshop activity for homework, and conduct response on the following day.
- If students need increased support, they can work in pairs or small groups during workshop and you can conduct response as a whole class activity.
- With younger students, limit the literature models. You may want to give all students the same literature model. With older students, encourage more independence over a wider range of materials.

Lesson 4: Beginning Hooks

Objective: Students will learn several techniques for writing an opening hook.

Materials: Literature models, newspapers, content-area textbooks and/or non-fiction magazines, *Beginning Hooks with Examples* (see page 94) for each student, writers' notebooks

Mini-Lesson (20-25 minutes)

Now that your students have discussed and practiced determining a focus for an expository piece and writing main idea statements for body paragraphs, they are ready to learn about beginning their introductory paragraphs. Explain that the function of the introductory paragraph is to hook the reader's attention and to introduce the focus of the piece. Read various opening hooks to students from *Beginning Hooks with Examples* and from literature models. Talk about the general types of hooks writers use:

- Question
- Onomatopoeia
- Exclamations
- Startling fact
- Voice
- Definition
- General to specific statement
- Riddle
- Quotation
- Anecdote
- Idiom
- Sentence fragments

Arrange students in groups of three or four and direct them to search magazine articles, newspaper articles, and textbook chapters for examples of hooks. Of course, they will refer to the beginning of each article or chapter. (Students can record hooks on sentence strips or index cards if you would like to physically sort the beginning hooks as extra support for students.) After about five minutes, allow each group to share the hooks they located. Lead students in a discussion about the types of hooks found and help classify them.

Workshop (10 minutes)

Distribute copies of *Beginning Hooks with Examples* for students to store in the resource section of their writers' notebooks. Students will use the graphic organizer for which they determined a focus in the previous lesson to practice writing beginning hooks. Instruct each student to write three different types of hooks for this piece. Circulate and assist, informally assessing their mastery of the skill.

Response (5-10 minutes)

Ask each student to share one beginning hook with the class and have the class identify the type of hook used. Affirm student responses and clarify misconceptions.

Modifications

- If time is limited, conduct the mini-lesson in class and assign the workshop activity as homework. Be sure to conduct response in class the following day.
- If students need increased support, they can work in small groups to write beginning hooks.
- If you prefer, response can be conducted in the form of peer conferences. However, be sure to observe each student to assess levels of mastery.
- Collect the lists of hooks students found during the mini-lesson and compile a meaningful, student-made resource for students to keep in their writers' notebooks.
- Encourage your students to create and create and maintain their own on-going lists of beginning hooks to keep in the resource sections of their writers' notebooks.
- If students have difficulty recognizing or classifying hooks, extend the modeling portion of the mini-lesson before moving on to workshop.

Lesson 5: Hunting for Transitional Phrases

Objective: Students will create lists of transitional phrases found in expository texts.

Materials: Literature models, newspaper articles, non-fiction magazine articles, content-area textbooks, writers' notebooks

Mini-Lesson (10 minutes)

It is important that students understand how to link paragraphs and ideas together using transitional phrases. Transitional phrases form the connection between ideas. Young students learn to use transitional words, such as *first, next, finally*...to move from one sub-topic to another within a piece. As students mature, transitional phrases should mature as well. Some common types of transitional phrases are

- Additions (*for instance, another thought, in addition to...*)
- Alternatives (*on the other hand, in some cases, whereas, but...*)
- Comparisons (*similarly, unlike, when compared to, like...*)
- Incidence (*always, usually, frequently, occasionally, sometimes, never...*)
- Cause and Effect (*as a result, because, consequently...*)
- Emphasis (*once again, to repeat, to reiterate, for this reason...*)
- Summarization (*in closing, the last thing, finally, to sum it up...*)

Select a literature model from which to read a variety of well-crafted transitional phrases. Age-appropriate magazines and many non-fiction books are ideal, but you may also find good transitional phrase models in content-area textbooks. Discuss the function of different transitional phrases and how mature, well-written transitions provide seamless connections and natural flow.

Workshop (20-25 minutes)

Direct students to scan many pieces of expository text, searching for and recording well-crafted transitional phrases. If you are able to bring multiple resources into your classroom for this purpose, this activity can be done on site. However, you will probably experience better success with this lesson if you make arrangements with the media specialist to take students to the media center for a transitional phrase hunt. Students can work in teams of two or three to scan non-fiction books and magazines for transitional phrases. Each team should have a recorder who maintains a list of phrases found by the group. Be sure to set a time limit for this activity (about 15 minutes).

Response (5-10 minutes)

Each group should report by either reading their list of transitional phrases, or if time is limited, selecting their three favorites to share. Discuss the type and function of each phrase to be sure students understand how to use it correctly. Collect these lists and compile them into a master list of transitional phrases to reproduce and distribute to students for the resource section of their writers' notebooks.

Modifications

- If time is limited, prepare students one day by conducting the mini-lesson and a modified transitional phrase hunt within the classroom so that they understand the process and expectations. The next day, visit the media center for the actual transitional phrase hunt.
- If time is limited and you cannot afford to devote two days to this lesson, students can complete the transitional phrase hunt as a homework activity. However, students will probably have a far more limited supply of resources, and this will diminish the effectiveness of the hunt.
- With younger students, you may want to assign specific sections of the media center to each group to refine the task and keep it from seeming overwhelming.
- If you would prefer to have each student create his or her own list of transitional phrases as a resource, conduct the response activity on the following day and have students write transitional phrases as they are shared.
- If students have limited experience with transitional phrases, select literature models and read them without the transitional phrases. You can have students provide transitional phrases and then compare them to the transitional phrases originally used by the author.
- As a follow-up, you can have students select transitional phrases that would fit the topic sentences they have already created for each clump of related details.

Lesson 6: Ending Techniques

Objective: Students will develop and practice techniques for composing conclusions.

Materials: Magazines/texts used during Lesson 4, writers' notebooks, graphic organizers used in Lesson 3

Mini-Lesson (15-20 minutes)

Ending techniques are a little more difficult than beginning hooks. Before adding a conclusion, writers need to examine the supporting details presented in the piece to be sure that all evidence leads logically to the conclusion. There are some basic ending techniques to present to students:

- Universal word ending *(all, everyone, ...)*
- Sum up the facts and state the message *(to sum it up, let's review...)*
- Circle back to the hook
- Give the reader advice *(I can tell you this, if you...)*
- Make a comparison
- State a lesson learned or major character change *(one thing I learned, ...)*

Use literature models to provide examples of each type of ending technique. Arrange students in groups of three or four, using the same magazines, newspapers, and content-area textbooks as in Lesson 4. This time, instead of looking for beginning hooks, students will look for ending techniques used in these texts. Set a time limit, about 5-7 minutes, for groups to compile ending techniques. When time is up, each group should share the examples they found. Classify the types of ending techniques located.

Workshop (10-15 minutes)

Students will need the graphic organizers for which they determined a focus in Lesson 3. During workshop, students will work independently to create three different possible conclusions for this piece, using three of the ending techniques listed above. Circulate and assist students during workshop, informally assessing understanding and mastery.

Response (10 minutes)

Ask volunteers to share one or more of the conclusions they created and state the type of ending technique used. Provide positive reinforcement and clarify misconceptions. These endings may seem unnatural and contrived, because they are not being written at the end of an actual piece. However, this practice provides experience that leads to well-crafted conclusions when students do actually come to the end of a written piece.

Modifications

- If time is limited, conduct the mini-lesson one day and conduct workshop and response on the following day.
- If students have difficulty employing ending techniques independently, back up and work on creating conclusions together as a shared writing activity.
- If students need moderate support, allow them to work as partners.
- Response can be conducted as peer conferences as long as you feel that students have enough command over the concept of ending techniques to recognize and discuss them in that setting.
- You may want to compile the conclusions students located in texts to create a meaningful, student-made resource.
- If students create well-crafted conclusions, collect them to make a class resource of examples of types of ending techniques. Resources that come from the students can have more of an impact than those from outside sources.

Lesson 7: Organizing Steps to a Process

Objective: Students will create and arrange steps to a process in sequential order.

Materials: Process prompts, how-to literature model, writers' notebooks

Mini-Lesson (10-15 minutes)

Provide a process prompt on the board for which you have a literature model on hand. (See page 93 for a sample process paper, *"How to Upholster a Chair."*) Do not read the sample out loud. Begin with the prompt, and ask students to furnish steps to the process. Write them on the board, leaving space between each in order to insert steps as needed. Think out loud to model the thought processes for reviewing, ordering, and inserting steps. When students feel satisfied that they have thought of all necessary steps, read the literature model and compare it with the steps on your list. Discuss differences between the how-to piece and other expository writing: how-to pieces are sometimes written in future tense and are often written in second person, speaking directly to the reader.

Workshop (15 minutes)

Provide another process prompt for students to use in creating steps (e.g., making a milkshake, hitting a baseball, studying for a test, cleaning a room). You may want to provide more than one prompt and allow students to select a prompt for which they have related experience. Students should work in partners for a predetermined amount of time (8-10 minutes). Each pair should discuss the process presented in the prompt and repeat the activity modeled during the mini-lesson, listing steps, leaving spaces between each, reviewing, ordering, and inserting steps as needed. The keys to organizing a how-to piece are specificity of details and sequential order. Circulate, observe, and assist students as needed during workshop.

Response (5-10 minutes)

Each pair should read their set of ordered steps. If the whole class had the same prompt, compare similarities and differences. Look for thoroughness and question omissions. Provide specific praise for thorough, sequential lists.

Modifications

- If time is limited, present the mini-lesson on one day and the workshop/response portion on the following day.
- Students might prefer to generate a list of process prompts after the mini-lesson. You can use this list for the workshop activity and later assignments.
- If students need increased support, begin the workshop activity as a whole group and allow partners to complete the steps as a workshop activity.
- For younger students, you can distribute index cards for the workshop activity. This will assist them in sequencing steps, especially when insertions are made.

Lesson 8: Assessment

Objective: Students will demonstrate mastery of creating an organizational template for an expository piece and planning sequential steps to a process.

Materials: Two expository prompts (one process prompt and one other), writers' notebooks

Mini-Lesson (5 minutes)

Review the difference between organizing details for a process prompt and for all other expository prompts. Display the graphic organizers introduced in Lesson 2a and review directions for using each.

Assessment (30 minutes)

Provide students with two expository prompts (one process prompt and one other). Students will create two plans for writing. For the process prompt, they will create a list of at least ten steps in sequential order. For the other prompt, they will create a list of details, choose and draw a graphic organizer, and create clumps of related details. For each clump, students must write a brief rationale (one to four words). Additionally, students should determine a focus for the entire piece.

Scoring

You can use either a rubric or a weighted checklist to score student papers, depending upon your needs and preferences. (The process for using a weighted checklist is just like using the weighted checklist in the previous chapter, with the new objectives added.) A sample of each is provided on page 41. You can also create two separate rubrics for the two different prompts, especially if you elect to make the modification of providing the two prompts on separate days.

Save these plans for a future writing assignment during Step Three. Do not write evaluation information or grades directly on the graphic organizer or detail list. Instead, use a rubric or checklist for all grades and comments. Students can keep the plans in their writers' notebooks or you can be responsible for saving them until they are needed.

If most students are able to move on to the next step but one or two still have difficulty competently demonstrating these skills, you may want to provide some extra assignments as differentiated instruction for these students.

Students who have not mastered these objectives would benefit from

- Taking a graphic organizer you have created and working backwards through the steps to the list of details.
- Working on a prepared graphic organizer with half of the details in both the list and the organizer in place and half left blank for them to complete.
- Creating a detail list and graphic organizer in a peer-assisted learning activity.

Modifications

- You can conduct the assessment in two different sessions, presenting a general expository prompt prior to Lesson 7 and a process prompt after Lesson 7.
- You can divide the lesson into two parts on consecutive days, with a review and practice on one day and the assessments on the following day.

- You can provide several prompts and allow students to choose the prompts they will use for this assessment, as long as one is a process prompt and the other is not.
- You can provide students with copies of the rubric or weighted checklist in advance, and as they complete the assignment, they can assess themselves. This will help them stay focused on the objectives as they work.

> Optional Lesson Ideas

- Detail and organization lessons blend nicely with note-taking (a skill critical to success in secondary school and higher education, yet not directly taught and practiced in many cases). Students can practice taking notes in the form of pertinent details and clumping them into related groups or rewriting them in outline form. You can use a content-area lesson, a video, or a presentation as the basis for this activity.
- Book reports on short non-fiction books are a great way to reverse the graphic organizer process for deeper understanding. Students can read the text and then transfer the information onto a graphic organizer, clumping related details from the text and establishing the rationale or main idea for each clump of details.
- Ask students to analyze short expository texts and identify a beginning hook, transitional phrases, sub-topics, supporting details, an ending technique, and the overall focus of a newspaper or magazine article.
- When moving from graphic organizer to a written piece, students will have to decide the order of their paragraphs. Once they have created graphic organizers from their detail lists, you can teach students to order their paragraphs. If the information presented is historical, the order may be apparent. When presenting other information, students need to make decisions about the order of presentation. Offer these ideas. *within three body paragraphs, put the paragraph with the weakest support in the middle; put the most critical information first, concrete examples second, and reminders last; write your best-supported body paragraph first to make a good impression on the reader and to be sure it is written in case you run out of time during a timed writing assessment.*
- Practice the organization of a process paper by having students develop and write a recipe. This can be an actual recipe or a humorous concoction. Students do not have to write the recipe in paragraph form, but can extend it to an enumerated list of sentences providing sequential directions.
- If you are looking for a creative, hands-on project to review skills and provide practice in sequencing steps of a process, allow students to invent a game and write a set of directions to go with it. A game comprised of writing skills makes a good review; a game reviewing or practicing content-area information and skills is a great way to integrate subject areas.
- You can prepare a graphic organizer or sequential list with many items left blank. Students can fill in the missing details or steps to complete the plan.
- Students can take another field trip to the media center to search for and collect beginning hooks or ending techniques, the way they hunted for transitional phrases in Lesson 5.
- A class newsletter is a great way to practice and apply organizational skills. Students can create a template for their newsletter, with designated sections for different types of information (e.g., *new skills, homework, spotlight on success, etc.).*

> Pausing to Create a Written Piece

A writing sample at this point would be assessed based upon the skills taught and learned, along with one or two writing conventions you have taught and for which you can hold students responsible.

For example, students can use the graphic organizer developed in Lesson 7 and compose a complete process-writing piece. Use a rubric or weighted checklist to assess students on the following skills: supporting details, organization, focus, beginning hook, transitional phrases, ending technique, and one or two conventions, such as capitalization and end punctuation.

To assess competency, use a rubric like the sample supplied on page 41, substituting the above skills as the objectives. If you want to use a weighted checklist, each of the objectives could be given the value of five points, to build upon the sixty points allotted for completing the assignment.

If you pause to have students create a written piece at this point, save it to use as a sample for revision and editing activities at a later time. Students benefit from going back to their own writing to identify areas for improving craft.

Sample Rubric—Organization

Name:____**Date:**______________________

Target Skills: The student is able to 1) create thorough detail lists; 2) clump related details on a graphic organizer; 3) establish a rationale for each group; 4) determine a focus; and 5) create a thorough, sequential list of steps to a process.

Objectives	**3** Applies skills competently and creatively.	**2** Applies skills competently.	**1** Attempts to apply skills.	**0** Does not apply skills.
Creates a thorough detail list.				
Clumps related details on a graphic organizer.				
Establishes a rationale for each group.				
Determines an overall focus for the piece.				
Creates a thorough, sequential list of steps to a process.				

Sample Weighted Checklist—Organization

Name:____**Date:**________________

Target Skills: The student is able to 1) create thorough detail lists; 2) clump related details on a graphic organizer; 3) establish a rationale for each group; 4) determine a focus; and 5) create a thorough, sequential list of steps to a process.

______Completes assignment (60)

______Creates thorough lists of details (10)

______Clumps details into related groups (10)

______Establishes rationale for each group and a focus for the piece (10)

______Arranges steps to a process in sequential order (10)

CHAPTER FOUR

Step Three—Writing Expository Paragraphs

> Paragraph Form

Students at this level have been taught and have practiced paragraph form. They should know how to write a topic sentence, and for the most part, they should have developed sentence fluency, or the ability to compose complete sentences with syntactical flow.

If students have not mastered writing paragraphs with topic sentences, related details, and sentence fluency, you may want to provide some basic paragraphing lessons and practice before proceeding with the skills introduced in this chapter.

You will introduce and provide practice for different types of paragraph progression and focus in order to create well-crafted, mature paragraphs that deliver a cohesive message to the reader. The types of expository paragraphs addressed in this chapter are

- Comparison
- General-to-Specific
- Specific-to-General
- Cause-and-Effect
- Question-and-Answer
- Introduction
- Conclusion

Two common and valuable types of paragraphs omitted from this chapter are sequential paragraphs and problem/solution paragraphs. The problem and solution format is most often used in persuasive writing, which is covered in a different book. Sequential paragraphs are essential to how-to writing and are often used in writing that recounts historical events. Students have already practiced sequential paragraphs in Step Two when they developed a response to a process prompt.

If you determine you need to provide further practice for sequential paragraphs, feel free to add a lesson. Students can develop an ordered list of details as a plan. While writing, a new lesson focus can be the use of time-order transitional phrases.

> Literature Models

As each type of paragraph is introduced, you will need to provide literature models. You can look through magazines, newspapers, non-fiction books, and content-area textbooks to begin collecting literature models as preparation for teaching this step. As you complete this step, you can also save student samples. From year to year, your collection of literature models will grow.

There are some terrific resources available from the CraftPlus® collection as well. *Listen to This: Developing an Ear for Expository* is a collection of read-aloud samples of expository works. In it, Marcia Freeman offers tips for sharing expository samples with students. Additionally, this book provides a wealth of short expository pieces by various authors.

Another great resource is *Models for Teaching Writing-Craft Target Skills*. This CraftPlus companion book lists trade books and educational materials that demonstrate specific writing-craft skills. Information about both of these CraftPlus resources can be found in the bibliography of this book.

Once students have been introduced to these paragraph types, they can also become resources, bringing specific paragraph types to your attention from their own reading.

You will find it helpful to maintain a teacher notebook or crate of materials. File your resources behind dividers or in file folders. Save copies of literature models, lesson plans, and student samples from each lesson. As years pass, you will have an abundance of resources at your fingertips as you prepare to teach expository writing craft.

> Assessment

Students will be writing a great deal of connected text during this step. Assessment, therefore, will be ongoing and formative rather than culminating and summative.

Because you will be assessing competency throughout these lessons, you may want to use the *Paragraph Assessment Grid* on page 95 to record student achievement on each type of paragraph. This will provide you with valuable information at a glance, allowing you to determine if any particular lessons need to be repeated or extended, or if only certain individuals need targeted re-teaching and practice.

> Connected Text

This step bridges the gap between planning and drafting, the next step in the writing process. If you paused to have students complete a piece after Step Two, they have had recent practice writing connected text. Now they will not only produce connected text, but will learn how to craft their writing to deliver a desired message.

Variety of sentence structure is covered in this chapter as one of the Target Skills related to paragraph writing. Within any paragraph, across any genre, students need to avoid the repetition of sentence structure in order to keep the reader engaged and to avoid a stilted, formulaic presentation. Grammar lessons on compound and complex sentences may need to be reviewed with students. Hopefully, students have at least had experience with combining and extending sentences.

The main growth students should exhibit when going from emergent writer to fluent writer is the movement away from list-like sentences in a paragraph: *I have a dog. I have a cat. I have a turtle. My dog is brown. My cat is black. My turtle is green and brown.* The fluent writer can produce writing that is more connected and fluid: *I have three pets: a brown dog, a black cat, and a green turtle with brown spots.*

> Organization

Since we are focusing on specific paragraph types in this chapter, we will use some different organizational strategies. The graphic organizers and strategies used are not intended to be supports used for every paragraph a student writes within a multi-paragraph piece. Instead, they will draw attention to the thought processes inherent in designing these paragraph structures.

The organizational strategies and templates used in this chapter are designed to be an external manifestation of abstract thought processes. Be sure to "think out loud" as you organize details during a mini-lesson. Your modeling is key to your students' success.

The templates provided can also enhance your content-area instruction and reading comprehension exercises for non-fiction materials. Feel free to use these graphic organizers across the curriculum to dissect and understand expository text.

> Points to Remember

There are several different types of paragraphs introduced and practiced in this chapter. It would be very contrived and unnatural for your students to include each type in a piece of writing. However, understanding the structure of each type of paragraph is a tool for both well-crafted expository writing and reading comprehension.

When writing, students can develop details with a direct, meaningful focus. Also, they can revise a piece to add variety and stimulate interest simply by restructuring a paragraph within the piece. Naming these paragraph types provides language for you as you conference with students about ideas for possible revisions.

As you continue to read, either in read-aloud scenarios or in content-area textbook selections, encourage students to use their knowledge of paragraph types and names in your discussions. By doing so, you will reinforce writing skills and provide structure for comprehending expository text. Keep graphic organizers handy for dissecting text. You can make transparencies of the organizational templates provided on pages 89-92.

Students should keep the paragraphs they write during this step in their writers' notebooks. These will serve as springboards for revision and editing practice when we reach the final step in crafting expository papers.

> The Lessons

The lessons in this step involve more writing than students have done up to this point, with the exception of a possible complete piece written at the end of Step Two. One consideration when assigning paragraphs is that all students will not finish at the same time. It is advisable to have back-up activities for students who finish quickly. First, of course, they should read through their paragraphs to make improvements. If time remains, they can read through non-fiction books and magazines to locate literature models of the type of paragraph the class is writing.

Conversely, some students will not finish in the time allotted. To minimize procrastination, be sure to allocate a set time limit for students when writing. Posting a start and end time on the board, using a timer, or sticking a colorful arrow on the face of your classroom clock are all visual reminders of time limits for students as they work.

Because students are composing a great deal of independent writing, the talking stage of each lesson is very important. Students should be able to *try it out orally* before *trying it out in writing.* Talking will help them organize ideas and allows for some peer tutoring and clarifying questions.

At the beginning of Step Three, students will work to develop variety of sentence structure, a skill they can apply across genres. We will move from there into modeling and writing various types of paragraphs. Writing the introduction is saved for Lesson 7, as it's often easier to go back and write an introduction after the body of the piece has been developed. For this reason, students will probably benefit from thinking about the construction of an introductory paragraph after they have thought about and practiced the construction of various types of body paragraphs.

Lesson 1: Variety of Sentence Structure	Materials: Literature models, writers' notebooks	Objective: Students will learn to extend, expand, and combine sentences.
Lesson 2a: Comparison Planning	Materials: Literature model, writers' notebooks, large model and individual copies of *CraftPlus Comparison Analysis Organizer* (page 102)	Objective: Students will analyze a literature model and will collectively plan a comparison paragraph using the *CraftPlus Comparison Analysis Organizer.*
Lesson 2b: Comparison Paragraph	Materials: Literature model, writers' notebooks, *CraftPlus Comparison Analysis Organizer* developed in previous lesson	Objective: Students will write a comparison paragraph.
Lesson 3: General to Specific	Materials: Literature models, writers' notebooks, picture prompt	Objective: Students will design and write a deductive paragraph.
Lesson 4: Specific to General	Materials: Literature models, writers' notebooks	Objective: Students will design and write an inductive paragraph.
Lesson 5: Cause and Effect	Materials: Literature models, writers' notebooks	Objective: Students will design and write a cause-and-effect paragraph.
Lesson 6: Question and Answer	Materials: Literature models, writers' notebooks	Objective: Students will write a question-and-answer paragraph.
Lesson 7: Introduction	Materials: Literature models, writers' notebooks, a graphic organizer created during Step 2.	Objective: Students will design and write an introductory paragraph.
Lesson 8: Conclusion	Materials: Literature models, writers' notebooks	Objective: Students will design and write a conclusion.

Lesson 1: Variety of Sentence Structure

Objective: Students will learn to extend, expand, and combine sentences.

Materials: Literature models, writers' notebooks

Mini-Lesson (20 minutes)

Discuss sentence structure with your students. Remind them that a simple sentence has a subject and a predicate:

> *Dogs are mammals.*

Explain that while this simple sentence structure is effective, a reader would quickly become bored with a continuous string of simple sentences. Discuss the need for more complex sentences in order to break monotony.

Offer the example of a compound subject with a simple predicate:

> *Dogs and cats are mammals.*

Offer the example of a simple subject with a compound predicate (two verb phrases):

> *Dogs are mammals and are the most common domesticated animals.*

Allow students to offer examples of sentences with compound subjects and compound predicates. Next, introduce sentence combining to create compound sentences.

> *Dogs can be obedience trained. Cats rarely respond to behavior modification.*
>
> *Dogs can be obedience trained, but cats rarely respond to behavior modification.*

Combining sentences in this way is applicable to every genre, but works particularly well when making comparisons in expository text. Provide students with examples of paired simple sentences and allow students to orally combine them to create compound sentences. Finally, explain that simple sentences can also be improved through extension. For example:

Dogs are mammals.
Dogs are very common mammals.
Dogs are very common domesticated mammals.
Dogs are very common domesticated mammals with the potential to be trained.
According to experts, dogs are very common domesticated mammals with the potential to be trained.

This type of sentence extending triangle creates a powerful visual for students as they search for potential in extending sentences with greater detail and sophistication. Every sentence in a piece should not look like this, but some strategically placed extended sentences can break the monotony of rhythm and keep the reader engaged. Write a short, simple sentence on the board and work with students to extend it, one step at a time, as in the sentence-extending triangle above.

Workshop (15 minutes)

Have students generate a list of short, simple sentences. Write them on the board until you have a list of about twenty sentences. In their writers' notebooks, students should use these simple sentences to create one sentence with a compound subject, one sentence with a compound predicate, one compound sentence, and one sentence-extending triangle. Circulate and assist as needed.

Response (10 minutes)

Call on volunteers to share examples of each type of sentence. While all students may not share their sentences during response time, be sure you have read their examples during workshop and have informally assessed mastery of the skills being taught. As students share, be sure to respond with positive reinforcement and clarify any misconceptions.

Modifications

- If time is limited, present the mini-lesson one day and continue with workshop and response on the following day.
- If students need extra support, conduct the workshop as a partner-based or small-group activity.
- As a classroom resource, you may want to create a chart of various types of sentences from selected examples supplied by the students during response.
- If students have limited exposure and weak sentence fluency, break this lesson into four parts: compound subjects, compound predicates, compound sentences and the sentence-extending triangle.
- You can extend this activity to include other types of sentences, such as complex sentences and dialogue, or to include gerunds.

Lesson 2a: Comparison Planning

Objective: Students will analyze a literature model and will collectively plan a comparison paragraph using the *CraftPlus Comparison Analysis Organizer.*

Materials: Literature models, large model, and individual copies of the *CraftPlus Comparison Analysis Organizer* (see page 102), writers' notebooks.

Mini-Lesson (20-25 minutes)

Present a model of a comparison paragraph, such as:

> *Let the games begin! **Both** football and baseball are great American pastimes, inspiring loyalty among fans. They are **similar** in many respects, **but** each game has its own unique characteristics. **While** time segments are divided into four quarters during a football game, a baseball game runs the course of nine innings. Each quarter of a football game is measured to be a precise fifteen minutes of play. Baseball innings **however,** are indefinite in length. Each team gets its turn at bat during an inning, and remains at bat until accruing three outs. **Both** sports require team uniforms and the use of protective helmets. Football helmets are worn throughout the entire game. **On the other hand,** baseball helmets are only worn when a player is at bat. **Unlike** baseball players, football players must wear protective pads beneath their uniforms. Other than a player a bat, only a catcher is required to wear protective pads and equipment in a baseball game. The games are **similar** in that they each have a scoring system, and scores are made when a player crosses a boundary. In football, the player must carry the ball across the goal line, scoring six points (with the opportunity to score one or two extra points every time a goal is made). Football also allows for other scoring options, like the three-point field goal. **In contrast,** there is only one way to score in baseball: one run is scored each time a player reaches home plate safely. **Both** games require offensive and defensive tactics, **but** football players generally only play one or the other, **whereas** baseball players are required to stay in the game for both offense and defense. Baseball players are often known as "the boys of summer," because the bulk of their official season occurs during the summer months. **Similarly,** football has its own season, beginning in the fall. **Just like** baseball, football season ends with a culminating championship game. Baseball's "World Series" championship is a sequence of up to seven games played in October; football comes to a close with one game, January's "Superbowl." **In both cases,** fans flock to stadiums and fill stands to cheer on the champs. Football and baseball may have their **differences,** but the excitement and emotion expressed by fans are the **same.** Take me out to the ballgame!*

After reading this comparison paragraph (or a comparison literature model), ask students to identify the cue words for comparison, like those bolded in the text above. (See page 51 for a more complete list.) Make a list of these cue words on the board, and have students make a comparison cue word list in their writers' notebooks to save as a reference. Use the words in the model and generate other cue words to add to them. Next, explain that the comparison paragraph is developed from attributes that show both similarities and differences. Such attributes can be developed on the well-known Venn diagram or on a *CraftPlus Comparison Analysis Organizer.* At this point in the lesson, help the students work backwards to draw comparison attributes from the model and list them on the organizer, like the sample provided on the next page.

CraftPlus® Comparison Analysis Organizer

Attributes	Football	Both	Baseball
Time	Quarter		Innings
Object	Ball over goal line	Goal destination	Player to home plate
Scoring	Six-point goal with a one- or two-point "extra point" option. Three-point field goal. Two-point safety.		Runs, one point each
Tactics	Tackling, blocking, intercepting	Offense/Defense	Force-outs, tags
Equipment	Pads	Ball, helmet	Caps, gloves, catcher's mask, and pads
Season	Fall/winter		Summer/fall
Championship	Superbowl, late January or early February, one game		World Series, October, up to seven games
Fans		Team loyalty, excitement, emotion	

Workshop (15 minutes)

After gaining an understanding of the planning process and the cue words used in comparison writing, develop an interactive comparison grid with your students. Post a large model on the board and provide students with individual copies of the *CraftPlus Comparison Analysis Organizer.* Work together to develop a comparison organizer using two other sports, two animals, two people, or any other meaningful objects of comparison for which the class can identify attributes and characteristics of similarity and difference.

Response (5 minutes)

Review the comparison literature model once more, to put the pieces back together. Draw attention to the new comparison grid completed collectively by the class and discuss options for opening hooks, comparison cue words, and other Target Skills that can be applied when writing the comparison paragraph.

Lesson 2b: Comparison Paragraph

Objective: Students will write a comparison paragraph.

Materials: *CraftPlus Comparison Analysis Organizers* created in the previous lesson, writers' notebooks

Mini-Lesson (10 minutes)

Review the *CraftPlus Comparison Analysis Organizers* created in the previous lesson. Discuss comparison cue words and add to the cue word reference lists if possible. Remind students of the possible beginning hooks generated during response in the previous lesson, and ask for new ideas for beginning hooks or ending techniques. Pair students and allow them to discuss ideas for writing their paragraphs for about five minutes.

Workshop (20-25 minutes)

Students will work independently to write a comparison paragraph. Students will include a beginning hook, comparison cue words, and an ending technique in their paragraphs. Additionally, you can set a discrete number of attributes to be addressed in the paragraph. For example, students are to address seven of the ten attributes listed on the collectively prepared organizer. This can be helpful if you are using the formative assessment option. Circulate and assist as needed during workshop.

Response (10 minutes)

Allow volunteers to share their comparison paragraphs with the class. Provide positive reinforcement and clarify misconceptions. Keep in mind that these paragraphs are in draft form. Feel free to make suggestions for revisions, but limit suggestions to one or two.

Assessment Option

Collect papers and score them according to a competency rubric (see page 99) or a weighted checklist that includes the requirements detailed in the workshop assignment. For example:

_____Completed assignment (60)

_____Beginning hook (10)

_____Seven attributes (10)

_____Comparison cue words (10)

_____Ending technique (10)

Modifications

- If you are not using the formative assessment option, you can allow students to work in pairs to create the paragraph as a peer-assisted learning activity.
- If time is limited, or if your students have minimal experience with comparison writing, you may want to slow the pace and present Lessons 2a and 2b over the course of three or fours days, rather than two.
- If students have a firm understanding of the organizer, you can allow them to select their own topics rather than developing an organizer together. If you choose to do this, conduct the development of the organizer as a tandem writing activity. You will work to develop attributes, similarities, and differences on your model organizer while the students work to develop their own.
- If you teach a content area as well as writing, you may want to integrate a science or social studies topic into this writing activity. Students can compare attributes of two animals, two countries, etc.
- If you would like to turn this workshop experience into a whimsical, creative activity, you can ask students to create their own items of comparison, such as two imaginary animals, two aliens, etc.

Cue Words for Comparison

also
although
and
both
but
comparatively
different
differs
dissimilar
equally
in contrast
like
maybe
on the other hand
opposites
or
same as
similar(ly)
unlike
yet

Lesson 3: General to Specific

Objective: Students will design and write a deductive paragraph.

Materials: Literature model, writers' notebooks, picture prompt

Mini-Lesson (15-20 minutes)

Deductive reasoning works from the general to the specific. This type of paragraph is very typical, with a main idea statement presented first, followed by details to support that statement. (The opposite approach is inductive, which will be presented in the succeeding lesson. The two lessons should be tied together to help students understand these inverse processes of reasoning and writing.) To present this lesson, begin by sharing a literature model with a general-to-specific progression, easily found in content-area textbooks, or in newspapers and magazines. After sharing one or two literature models, present a general topic sentence to the class. For example:

> *Fall is a time of change.*

Ask students to present details or observations that would support this statement.

For example:

General Statement	Specific Details
Fall is a time of change.	• *Changing color of leaves* • *Thinning appearance of trees* • *Migration of many bird species* • *Cooling temperatures* • *Grass and plants becoming brown and dry* • *Shorter days* • *Revert to standard time*

Explain to students that the structure of the deductive paragraph goes from general to specific. Work with students to turn this statement and list of supporting details into a model paragraph. Allow students to offer sentences as you write them. Encourage and reinforce the use of composing skills (onomatopoeia, metaphor, strong verbs, rich vocabulary, voice, etc.) and variation in sentence structure. When complete, the paragraph should be closed with a confirmation of the thesis supported by the details and observations. The completed paragraph might look like this:

> *Fall is a time of change. Everywhere you look, various shades of red, yellow, orange, and brown have replaced the green once seen blanketing trees. Branches become more apparent as leaves begin to dry and fall. You can hear the crunch of dead leaves and brown grass beneath your feet as you walk. Cooling temperatures and shorter days signal the migration of many bird species to warmer climates. In late October, clocks are turned back one hour in a return to standard time. You can look at the changes around you and see that fall has arrived.*

Read over the model paragraph together and review the structure of general to specific.

Workshop (20 minutes)

Present students with a picture prompt and a general statement about the picture, such as:

Chicago is truly the windy city.

Such a sentence, provided along with a picture of Chicago exhibiting the effects of wind, forms a generalization for students to support with evidence from the picture. Have students list at least five observations and details in the picture to support the topic sentence. After a few minutes of listing, stop to share evidence students have found in the picture to support the statement. Students may add to their lists during this time. Next, assign the paragraph. Students are to begin with the topic sentence, present the evidence, and end with a confirmation of the thesis. Circulate and assist while students write.

Response (5-10 minutes)

Ask volunteers to share their paragraphs. Remember that the target is writing a paragraph that moves from general to specific, and ends with a confirmation of the thesis. Be sure to address this pattern as each paragraph is read. You can also reinforce sentence variation and the application of composing skills at this time.

Assessment Option

If you are using the formative assessment option, collect and score paragraphs. Keep in mind that this is a rough-draft effort. You can use a competency rubric to assess the level of mastery (see page 99 for an example), or you can use a weighted checklist if you need to derive a percentage. For example:

_____Complete (60)
_____Begins with general statement (10)
_____Specific evidence supports general statement (10)
_____Ends with confirmation of general statement (10)
_____Sentence variation and craft (10)

Modifications

- If you are not using the formative assessment option, you can allow students to work in pairs or small groups to complete the workshop assignment.
- If your students are accustomed to paragraph writing and Target Skills, you should be able to complete this lesson within the time suggested. However, if your students need a slower pace and more scaffolding, stretch the lesson over the course of two days and increase the level of modeling and interaction.
- If your time is limited, present the mini-lesson one day and complete the workshop and response sections on the following day.
- If time is limited, you can assign the workshop portion as homework, but students would need a copy of the picture prompt. In this case, you may choose to provide separate picture prompts to each student.
- If you do not have a potent picture prompt, you can use an interesting object or go outside for a natural observation.
- Integrate different subject areas by supplying a general statement related to a science or social studies topic.
- As a response activity, you can have students conduct peer conferences instead of sharing a few pieces with the entire class.

Lesson 4: Specific to General

Objective: Students will design and write an inductive paragraph.

Materials: Literature models, writers' notebooks, picture prompts, and detail lists from previous lesson

Mini-Lesson (15-20 minutes)

Explain to students that inductive reasoning moves from specific to general. It is the inverse of the deductive process, and can create nice variety in paragraph format. Read one or two literature models of inductive paragraph structure (often found in magazines and personal interest news stories). To create a class model, use the topic sentence and details from the previous mini-lesson. For example:

Fall is a time of change.

- *Changing color of leaves*
- *Thinning appearance of trees*
- *Migration of many bird species*
- *Cooling temperatures*
- *Grass and plants becoming brown and dry*
- *Shorter days*
- *Revert to standard time*

Work with students to turn the topic sentence and details into a paragraph that moves from the specific to the general. For example:

> *Crunch, crunch! Can you hear the crackling of brown grass and dry leaves beneath your feet? Look around and see the various shades of red, yellow, orange, and brown where green once blanketed the trees. Notice that branches are more apparent now as leaves are falling from the trees. Darkness comes earlier, and in late October, clocks are turned back one hour in a transition back to standard time. Cooling temperatures signal the migration of many bird species. The evidence surrounds you: fall, a season of change, has arrived.*

Review the progression of specific to general. Compare this structure to the deductive paragraph created in the previous lesson.

Workshop (20 minutes)

Present students with the picture prompt used in the previous lesson. Have students open their writers' notebooks to the list of details and observations they made about the picture prompt. Instruct students to use these same details to write an inductive paragraph, moving from specific details to a general statement or thesis. Circulate and assist as needed.

Response (5-10 minutes)

Allow volunteers to share their paragraphs with the class. Remember that the target is writing a paragraph that moves from specific to general, and ends with a statement of the main idea or thesis. Be sure to address this pattern as each paragraph is read. You can also reinforce sentence variation and the application of composing skills at this time.

Assessment Option

If you are using the formative assessment option, collect and score paragraphs. Keep in mind that this is a rough-draft effort. You can use a competency rubric to assess the level of mastery (see page 99 for an example), or you can use a weighted checklist if you need to derive a percentage. For example:

______Complete (60)

______Begins with hook and specific detail (10)

______Contains at least four supporting detail sentences (10)

______General statement at end (10)

______Sentence variation and craft (10)

Modifications

- If you are not using the formative assessment option, you can allow students to work in pairs or small groups to complete the workshop assignment.
- If your students are accustomed to paragraph writing and Target Skills, you should be able to complete this lesson within the time suggested. However, if your students need a slower pace and more scaffolding, stretch the lesson over the course of two days and increase the level of modeling and interaction.
- If time is limited, you can present the mini-lesson one day and present the workshop and response portions on the following day.
- Integrate subjects by using a science or social studies topic for this paragraph.
- The workshop portion can be assigned as homework as long as students have a copy of the picture prompt. In this case, you may choose to use separate picture prompts for each student.
- If you do not have a potent picture prompt, you can use an interesting object or go outside for a natural observation.
- As a response activity, you can have students conduct peer conferences instead of sharing a few pieces with the entire class.

Lesson 5: Cause and Effect

Objective: Students will design and write a cause-and-effect paragraph.

Materials: Literature models, writers' notebooks

Mini-Lesson (15-20 minutes)

Cause-and-effect paragraphs follow the common format of the deductive paragraph: a topic sentence followed by supporting details. The cause-and-effect paragraph, however, is intended to "explain why" and is well-suited for prompts of this nature. Present one or two literature models of cause-and-effect paragraphs. Point out the effect stated in the topic sentence and ask students to recount the details presented as causes. Next, present an effect to students. For example:

> *Childhood obesity is a growing trend in the America.*

Ask students to provide causes for this effect and list them on the board. For example:

Effect	Possible Causes
Rise in childhood obesity	- *Decreased time in physical education classes* - *Decrease in or elimination of recess during school* - *Growing popularity and availability of video games and computers* - *Wider availability of television programming directed at children* - *Increase in fast food consumption* - *Decrease in family dinners among American families*

Work with students to create a cause-and-effect paragraph from this topic sentence and list of supporting details. Encourage the use of sentence variation and composing skills. As you write, be sure to include and call attention to cause-and-effect cue words. For example:

> *Childhood obesity is a growing trend in America today. There are several* ***reasons*** *for this phenomenon. The growing popularity and availability of video games and computers may* ***cause*** *a decrease in activity. A growing number of television programs directed at children may also keep kids sitting still instead of moving.* ***As a result,*** *kids are getting less exercise. Some people point to changes in eating habits as the main culprit. Fewer families are eating home-cooked meals together.* ***Instead,*** *busy families often rely on fast food, which is generally high in fat and calories. As schools reach for higher academic standards, recess and physical education time have diminished, or in some cases disappeared, for young students.* ***Consequently,*** *children are getting less activity in school as well as at home. Without a doubt, there are many factors contributing to the dangerous rise in childhood obesity.*

Cause-and-effect cue words are bolded in the paragraph above. Some common cause-and-effect cue words are

since	because	as a result
therefore	due to	consequently
for this reason	cause	in response
which caused	so	that's why

Workshop (20 minutes)

Provide students with another general effect statement, such as:

> *Many schools are adopting the policy of school uniforms.*

Students should list possible causes of this effect in their writers' notebooks. After a few minutes, allow students to share their ideas with the class. Be careful to distinguish between causes and effects. For instance, disparity of clothing among students from different socio-economic backgrounds can be considered a cause of this effect. However, students protesting uniform policies would not be a cause; it would be an effect. Once you have heard ideas and clarified misconceptions, direct students to write their cause-and-effect paragraphs. Tell them to use the topic sentence provided, offer at least four causes, use cause-and-effect cue words, and end with a concluding sentence. Circulate and assist as needed while students are writing.

Response (5-10 minutes)

Allow volunteers to share their paragraphs with the class. Remember that the target is writing a paragraph that begins with a topic sentence stating effect, presents at least four possible causes of the effect, uses cause-and-effect cue words, and ends with a concluding sentence. Be sure to address this pattern as each paragraph is read. You can also reinforce sentence variation and the application of composing skills at this time.

Assessment Option

If you are using the formative assessment option, collect and score paragraphs. Keep in mind that this is a rough-draft effort. You can use a competency rubric to assess the level of mastery (see page 99 for an example), or you can use a weighted checklist if you need to derive a percentage.

For example:

_____Complete (60)
_____Opens with hook and specific detail (10)
_____Presentation of at least four other specific details (10)
_____General statement at end (10)
_____Sentence variation and craft (10)

Modifications

- If you are not using the formative assessment option, you can allow students to work in pairs or small groups to complete the workshop assignment.
- If your students are accustomed to paragraph writing and Target Skills, you should be able to complete this lesson within the time suggested. However, if your students need a slower pace and more scaffolding, stretch the lesson over the course of two days and increase the level of modeling and interaction.
- If time is limited, you can present the mini-lesson one day and present the workshop and response portions on the following day.
- Integrate subjects by using a science or social studies topic for this paragraph.
- As a response activity, you can have students conduct peer conferences instead of sharing a few pieces with the entire class.

Lesson 6: Question and Answer

Objective: Students will write a question-and-answer paragraph.

Materials: Literature models, writers' notebooks

Mini-Lesson (15-20 minutes)

The question-and-answer paragraph format can often be found in content-area textbooks, newspaper articles, and informational magazine articles. Read one or two models of this paragraph format to students at the beginning of the lesson as an introduction. Explain that this paragraph style works well with "explain why" and "explain how" prompts. After reading literature models, begin to build an interactive model writing plan with the students by presenting a question. Select a topic from recent content-area studies, or from any topic with which your students are well acquainted. For example:

> *Have you ever wondered why the Pilgrims chose to make the difficult journey to America?*

Next, have students offer answers and list them in a bulleted fashion. For example:

Question	Possible Answers
Why did Pilgrims come to America?	- *religious persecution, Church of England vs. Separatists* - *rule of monarchy* - *wanted to find farming community* - *wanted children to continue language and customs of parents (problem with Holland)* - *opportunity with London Company*

At this point, you have modeled paragraph construction with your students a few times. Allow your students to talk through sentence structure ideas. Develop ideas for an ending technique that supplies a general statement to "sum up" the response. Remind students to apply writing-craft skills and use a variety of sentence structure.

Workshop (20 minutes)

Students will work independently to construct a paragraph from the interactive plan. They should begin with the question you have posted on the board and supply supporting details in the form of answers. Circulate and assist as needed.

Response (5-10 minutes)

Allow volunteers to share their paragraphs. Positively reinforce the development of the question-and-answer format, variety of sentence structure, and application of writing-craft skills. Be sure to clarify misconceptions.

Assessment Option

If you are using the formative assessment option, collect and score paragraphs. Keep in mind that this is a rough-draft effort. You can use a competency rubric to assess the level of mastery (see page 99 for an example), or you can use a weighted checklist if you need to derive a percentage. For example:

_____Complete (60)

_____Opens with question (10)

_____Presentation of at least four answers (10)

_____General statement at end (10)

_____Sentence variation and craft (10)

Modifications

- If students need more modeling and support, you can use the plan created in the mini-lesson for an interactive modeling activity, and assign a different question for students to use for planning and writing during workshop.
- If you are not using the assessment option, students can work in pairs or small groups to complete the paragraph. In this scenario, you may want to give each group a different question for which to plan and write a question-and-answer paragraph.
- You can easily make this an integrated activity by using a current science or social studies topic as the question.
- As a response activity, you can have students conduct peer conferences instead of sharing a few pieces with the entire class.

Lesson 7: Introduction

Objective: Students will design and write an introductory paragraph.

Materials: Literature models, writers' notebooks, class model of a graphic organizer created in Step Two, Lesson 2a, graphic organizer created during Step Two, Lesson 8.

Mini-Lesson (15-20 minutes)

Explain to students that the general function of the introductory paragraph is to hook the reader's attention and introduce the topic. More specifically, the purpose might be to:

- Give background information
- Tell how you got interested in the subject
- Tell how you feel about the subject
- Set a tone or atmosphere
- Tell why the topic is important to the reader
- Define the topic
- State a problem
- Tell what you want
- State your position on an issue

The specific purpose of the introductory paragraph depends on the topic. Regardless of the topic, there are two types of introductory paragraphs students should learn to write. The traditional introductory paragraph outlines sub-topics to be addressed in the body of the paper. For example:

> *Stop! Before you open that refrigerator, you need to consider the rewards of healthy food choices. When you make good choices about what goes into your body, you will reap many benefits, including longevity, quality of life, and the modeling of sound nutritional choices for your family members. Be sure to choose wisely.*

In modern writing, this type of introductory paragraph is often viewed as unnatural and formulaic. The CraftPlus curriculum encourages students to depart from this format by eliminating the preview of sub-topics and moving more quickly into the body of the paper. For example:

> *Stop! Before you open that refrigerator, you need to consider the rewards of healthy food choices. When you make good choices about what goes into your body, you will reap many benefits...so be sure to choose wisely.*

Present both types of introductory paragraphs to your students and discuss their preferences as readers. Encourage them to write the CraftPlus model, but make sure they are exposed to and know how to write the traditional format, in case they are ever required to do so.

Although introductory paragraphs appear at the beginning of a piece, they are best written last. In order to capture the focus of the piece in the first two or three sentences, a writer must have completed the body and be well acquainted with the details, tone, and direction of the entire piece.

Review the various types of beginning hooks commonly used in expository text. (Students should have *Beginning Hooks with Examples* (page 94) stored in their writers' notebooks. They will it during this lesson.)

Display the graphic organizers modeled during Step Two, Lesson 2a. Review the supporting details and rationale for each clump of related details. Think out loud for students as you model the process of writing a beginning hook and introductory paragraph for one of these plans. Allow students to participate by offering ideas and suggestions.

Workshop (15-20 minutes)

Students will need the graphic organizers they created in Step Two, Lesson 8. During this workshop activity, they will create an introductory paragraph for one of their graphic organizers. Students will need to read over the supporting details and rationales for each clump of related details. Before writing, each student will need to decide on the type of beginning hook to be used, and determine the appropriate purpose of the introductory paragraph (listed above) in accordance with the topic. Circulate and assist as needed while students write their introductory paragraphs.

Response (5-10 minutes)

Allow volunteers to share their introductory paragraphs with the class. Reinforce the use of beginning hooks and clear purpose established in the introductory paragraphs.

Assessment Option

If you are using the formative assessment option, collect and score paragraphs. Keep in mind that this is a rough-draft effort. You can use a competency rubric to assess the level of mastery (see page 99 for an example), or you can use a weighted checklist if you need to derive a percentage.

For example:

_____Complete (60)
_____Opens with beginning hook (10)
_____Clearly introduces topic (10)
_____Establishes purpose (10)
_____Sentence variation and craft (10)

Modifications

- If time is limited, you can present the mini-lesson one day and continue with the workshop and response activities on the following day.
- If time is limited, you can present the mini-lesson in class and assign the workshop activity for homework.
- As a response activity, you can have students conduct peer conferences instead of sharing a few pieces with the entire class.
- Since a rationale has already been established for each of the clumps of related details, students can easily write a second introductory paragraph which introduces the sub-topics. In this case they can compare, contrast, and discuss preferences between the two styles of introductory paragraphs.
- If students need more support, conduct workshop as a tandem writing activity. Use a different plan and develop a beginning hook, thinking out loud. After you have written a hook, allow students time to write one. Next, develop a sentence that introduces the topic and establishes a purpose. With each step, think out loud and allow students to follow your model in their own writing.

Lesson 8: Conclusion

Objective: Students will design and write a conclusion.

Materials: Literature models, writers' notebooks

Mini-Lesson (15-20 minutes)

Begin by reading at least three or four concluding paragraphs from literature models. Magazine and newspaper articles are well suited for this purpose. Discuss elements of commonality among the models read. Explain that the ending of a piece needs to give the reader a sense of closure and satisfaction. There are several ending techniques commonly used by authors, including:

- Telling how you feel about the subject:

  I have developed a strong dislike for careless disposal of household wastes...
- Telling what you have learned:

  The effects of household garbage on the environment have taught me a very important lesson...
- Inviting the reader to learn more:

  If you would like to learn more about ways you can reduce household waste...
- Circling back to the hook:

  Grrrrmmmm! The garbage truck returns, but this time...
- Quoting an authority:

  Before you toss that jar in the trash can, remember the wise words of...
- Drawing a conclusion from the information presented:

  There's no doubt about it. All of these facts lead to the logical conclusion that...
- Reviewing the main points (traditional):

  Remember, there are three main reasons you should begin reducing household waste right away...

Discuss the types of ending techniques used in the models read. (Keep in mind that some conclusions may combine techniques.) Use the graphic organizer and introductory paragraph constructed during the previous lesson to model the formation of an ending paragraph. Discuss the ending technique you have chosen and explain your rationale. Think out loud as you write, and invite students to offer ideas and suggestions.

Workshop (20 minutes)

Students will use the graphic organizers and introductory paragraphs from the previous lesson to construct a concluding paragraph. The ending technique should be apparent, and the purpose established in the introductory paragraph should be clear in the conclusion. Circulate and assist as needed.

Response (5-10 minutes)

Allow volunteers to share their concluding paragraphs with the class. Have the class identify the ending technique used, and compare the conclusion to the introduction as a test for consistency of purpose and message.

Assessment Option

If you are using the formative assessment option, collect and score paragraphs. Keep in mind that this is a rough-draft effort. You can use a competency rubric to assess the level of mastery (see page 99 for an example), or you can use a weighted checklist if you need to derive a percentage. For example:

_____Complete (60)
_____Ending technique apparent (10)
_____Clearly addresses topic (10)
_____Purpose consistent with introductory paragraph (10)
_____Sentence variation and craft (10)

Modifications

- If time is limited, you can present the mini-lesson one day and continue with the workshop and response activities on the following day.
- If time is limited, you can present the mini-lesson in class and assign the workshop activity for homework.
- As a response activity, you can have students conduct peer conferences instead of sharing a few pieces with the entire class.
- Have students write a second concluding paragraph which reviews the sub-topics. In this case they can compare, contrast, and discuss preferences between the two styles.
- If students need more support, conduct workshop as a tandem writing activity. Use a different plan and develop a concluding paragraph. With each step, think out loud and allow students to follow your model in their own writing.
- If you are not using the assessment option, you can conduct response as a peer conference opportunity.

> Optional Lesson Ideas

- If you are not using the formative assessments throughout the lessons, you may want to conduct a summative assessment at this point. You can ask students to write one introductory paragraph, one body paragraph of their own choosing, and one concluding paragraph. Use a rubric to assess their proficiency with each type of paragraph.
- Students can complete a written piece by using the introductory paragraph and conclusion developed in these lessons, and adding three body paragraphs in the middle. You can assign three different types of paragraphs within the body of the piece if you like.
- You can assign a list of sentences for students to revise and expand.
- Play a sentence expansion game. Give each student a simple sentence on a piece of paper. Students will add one phrase to these sentences in order to extend them. Keep passing the sentences to different students. Each will add a phrase and pass the sentence on. After the sentences have been to about five students, stop and read them aloud.
- Students can interview each other and use interview data to practice writing paragraphs.
- Use the comparison and question/answer grids for science and social studies activities.
- You can add lessons about problem/solution paragraphs and sequential paragraphs if you want students to practice these paragraph structures.
- Make a class newspaper by assigning a type of paragraph to each student. Students should pick a topic (approved by the editor/teacher) and write that style of paragraph.

CHAPTER FIVE

Step Four—Writing an Expository Paper

> Putting It All Together

At this point, you have given your students all of the necessary components for writing a well-crafted expository paper. They should understand the primary importance of details, know how to create organization and structure, and possess techniques for composing purposeful paragraphs. Now they are ready to put the pieces together.

Teachers have often focused on the writing process without giving explicit instruction in the skills necessary for writing. Now that you have completed explicit instruction and meaningful practice, your students are ready for the writing process: prewriting, drafting, revising and editing. This step focuses on prewriting and drafting; the final step deals with revising and editing.

During Step Four, you will not teach new Target Skills. Instead, you will allow your students an opportunity to apply what they have learned. You will assign a piece of writing and you will set expectations for the specific skills that need to be present in that written assignment, such as:

Organizational	Composing	Conventions
• Detail list • Graphic organizer • Beginning Hook • Transitional Phrases • Ending Technique	• Sentence variation • Don't Hit Your Reader over the Head • Descriptive Attributes	• Indent paragraphs • Capital letters—I, proper nouns, beginnings of sentences

> Topics

If you are preparing your students to be assessed with prompts, you will probably want to supply an expository prompt instead of letting students choose their own topics. A sample list of expository prompts is included on page 97.

If your students are not regularly assessed with prompts, you may want to use a picture prompt, a content-area topic, or allow students to choose their own topics. Above all, be sure your students are writing about a topic that is within their realm of experience, a current course of study, or a subject of high interest.

> Assessment

Before you begin this series of lessons, you will need to determine your purpose and criteria for assessment. You may want to evaluate only the finished product, or you may want to assess students on their writing process skills.

You will also need to determine the type of assessment you will use. Sample rubrics and weighted checklists are provided on page 71-72. You may choose one of these, or you may create your own assessment instrument.

Be sure to decide upon your assessment instrument at the beginning of the lesson sequence and share it with the students. Students should understand the criteria and standards by which their papers will be scored.

> Points to Remember

While thoughtfully constructed, these expository pieces will be rough drafts that are not yet ready for publication. Remember, students have had opportunities to obtain feedback and make improvements throughout the process, but at this point you have not explicitly taught a system for revising and editing.

As you review these pieces, look for specific strengths and weaknesses. Jot down ideas for revision and editing. Look for trends across the entire group to help you focus your revision and editing lessons.

You can keep these genre-block pieces or have students store them in the rough draft section of their writers' notebooks. However, it is imperative that students have them available during the Step Five lessons. You are scoring these papers now as a rough draft, but you will soon score the same papers a second time as published work.

> The Lessons

This block of lessons is designed to be completed in four school days. If you need longer, feel free to alter the schedule. You will begin with detail lists, sort details into groups, and determine a rationale for each group. After that, students will begin writing.

Teach students that they can write a draft of the body paragraphs first, and then write the introduction and conclusion. Some students might be resistant to this idea, but if they try it, they will probably find the introduction much easier to write.

The teacher's role changes in this step. You become more of a facilitator than an instructor. Class time becomes more student-centered and less teacher-directed. You will review skills and procedures, and you will provide the assignment and criteria.

While the students are working, you will circulate and assist as needed. During response time, you will facilitate a discussion about the writing process and allow students to share parts of their compositions. However, the focal point of each day's lesson is composition.

Lesson 1: Listing and Clumping Details	Materials: Prompt or topic, graphic organizers, writers' notebooks	Objective: Students will create detail lists and clump details into related groups.
Lesson 2: Organizing Details and Writing Well-Supported Paragraphs	Materials: Writers' notebooks	Objective: Students will write a rationale for each group, create an outline by ordering the groups, and begin writing body paragraphs.
Lesson 3: Writing Well-Supported Paragraphs	Materials: Writers' notebooks	Objective: Students will continue writing body paragraphs.
Lesson 4: Writing an Introduction and Conclusion	Materials: Writers' notebooks	Objective: Students will write an introductory paragraph and a closing paragraph.

Lesson 1: Listing and Clumping Details

Objective: The students will create detail lists and clump details into related groups.

Materials: Prompt or topic, graphic organizers, writers' notebooks

Mini-Lesson (5 minutes)

Provide students with an expository prompt. (Select a prompt from page 97, provide a content-area prompt, use a picture prompt, or allow students to self-select a topic for writing.) Review the process for creating detail lists and clumping related details. Model if necessary.

Workshop (30 minutes)

Students will create detail lists, use a graphic organizer to clump related details together, and write a rationale for each group. You may assign the style of graphic organizer your students should use, or you may allow students to choose their own. Circulate and assist as needed. Be sure to check each student's work for wealth of details and logical clumping.

Response (5–10 minutes)

Allow volunteers to share their clumps of related details and begin to voice rationales for each group. Encourage students to compare and contrast detail lists and systems of organization.

Modifications

- To make this activity more concrete, you can provide sticky notes or index cards and allow students to physically sort details.
- If time is limited, you can assign the clumping portion of workshop for homework. However, it would be best for students to create detail lists under your supervision and guidance. (However, they can certainly add to the lists at home.) Response should be conducted at the beginning of the next lesson.
- For younger students, or for those in need of greater structure, you may want to provide a graphic organizer. For more mature writers, you will not need to provide a template.
- If students have difficulty creating detail lists, you can pause and allow students to meet in small groups for support and assistance.
- Response can be conducted in knee-to-knee peer conferences so that all students receive feedback.
- Response can be conducted in small groups, so that all students receive varied feedback.

Lesson 2: Organizing Details and Writing Well-Supported Paragraphs

Objectives: Students will write a rationale for each group, create an outline by ordering the groups, and begin writing body paragraphs.

Materials: Writers' notebooks, which should include work from the previous lesson.

Mini-Lesson (10 minutes)

Review the process for writing rationales, which become topic sentences, for each clump of related details. Review ideas for ordering paragraphs to create an outline for writing and determining a focus for the paper. Model if necessary.

Workshop (20 minutes)

Students should review their clumps of related details from the previous lesson and write a rationale for each group. After looking over the outline, students should be able to determine a clear focus for the paper. Once they have accomplished these tasks, students can begin drafting body paragraphs. Circulate and assist as necessary.

Response (10-15 minutes)

Pair students for peer conferences. Students will be at different points in the process, but will share their work with partners to receive one positive feedback comment and one suggestion for improvement, enhancement, or clarity.

Modifications

- If time is limited, students can conduct workshop as a homework assignment. Response should be conducted at the beginning of the following lesson. In this case, be sure to review each student's work since it will not be done under your supervision.
- Young students or students requiring additional structure can create a template for writing an outline, listing rationales, and determining a focus.
- Response can be conducted in small groups instead of pairs for more varied feedback.
- Response can be conducted in a whole-group setting if you need to maintain more control over the feedback provided.

Lesson 3: Writing Well-Supported Paragraphs

Objective: Students will continue writing body paragraphs.

Materials: Writers' notebooks, which should include work from the previous lesson.

Mini-Lesson (10 minutes)

Review the ordering of paragraphs with students. Offer suggestions for making decisions on paragraph order based upon the focus of the paper and the details included in each group. Review types of paragraphs. Read from models used in Step Three or have students share examples from their writers' notebooks as a reminder of the types of paragraphs they have learned and practiced. Encourage students to consider the overall focus of their papers and the types of details they are using to make decisions about paragraph types and paragraph order.

Workshop (20-25 minutes)

After carefully analyzing their focus, details, and rationales, students should work on ordering and crafting body paragraphs from each group of related details. Encourage students to concentrate on the body of the paper before writing the introduction. Circulate, observe, informally assess, and assist as needed.

Response (10 minutes)

Pair students for peer conferences with different partners than the last peer conference. Students will read their body paragraphs, receive feedback from partners, and then switch roles. Feedback should include at least one positive comment and one or two suggestions for improved craft or clarity. Circulate and monitor feedback.

Modifications

- If time is limited, you may assign the workshop activity as homework. However, be sure students have analyzed their groups of details to determine paragraph order and presentation style under your guidance.
- If students finish the body paragraphs, they may go on and write the introductory paragraph.
- You can conduct the response activity in small groups if you want to increase feedback.
- You can conduct the response activity as a whole class if you want to maintain greater control over feedback.
- You may need to model peer conferences again before launching the response activity.
- You can post examples of different paragraph types in the room so that students can see the models as they write.

Lesson 4: Writing an Introduction and Conclusion

Objective: Students will write an introductory paragraph and a closing paragraph.

Materials: Writers' notebooks, which should include the previous day's work.

Mini-Lesson (10 minutes)

Review beginning and ending techniques. Encourage students to use the resources in their writers' notebooks to review specific types of beginnings and endings. Review the functions of the first and last paragraph. Encourage students to write a beginning hook and introduce the topic, but also allow them to preview the sub-topics used in the body of the paper if they feel more comfortable doing so. Use a verbal model of both types of introductory paragraphs to refresh their memories. Stress that the preview of sub-topics is not necessary and its omission makes the introductory paragraph more enjoyable for the reader and less formulaic; however, make sure they *know* how to do it just in case they are ever *required* to do so.

Workshop (20-25 minutes)

Students should reread their body paragraphs and then begin to write their introductory paragraphs. Introductory paragraphs should include a beginning hook, state the topic, and establish the mood and focus of the paper. Closing paragraphs should employ one of the ending techniques learned during the previous step. Circulate, informally assess, and assist as needed.

Response (10 minutes)

Pair students for peer conferences with different partners than those used during the previous lesson. Model a peer conference if necessary. Students should read their completed papers to partners and receive feedback. Feedback should be comprised of one positive comment and one suggestion for improved craft or clarity. Circulate and monitor feedback.

Modifications

- If time is limited, students can begin writing in class and complete the workshop assignment at home. In this case, response should be conducted at the beginning of the next lesson.
- If time permits, students can work in small groups to listen to and provide feedback on their classmates' writing.
- Students may require modeling of the Target Skills at the beginning of the lesson.
- If necessary to produce quality work, allow two class periods for this assignment.

Sample Rubric for an Expository Rough Draft

Name:______________________________ **Date:**______________________________

Skills	**3** Applies skills competently and creatively.	**2** Applies skills competently.	**1** Attempts to apply skills.	**0** Does not apply skills.
Application of Organizational Skills				
Application of Composing Skills				
Application of Convention Skills				

Sample Rubric for Expository Writing Process

Name: ______________________________ **Date:**______________________________

Processes	**3** Applies skills competently and creatively.	**2** Applies skills competently.	**1** Attempts to apply skills.	**0** Does not apply skills.
Detail list				
Graphic organizer				
Completed rough draft				

Sample Weighted Checklist for Expository Rough Draft

Name:______________________________**Date:**_______________**Score:**______________

_____ Complete (60)

_____Detail list (5) _____ Graphic Organizer (5)

_____Don't Hit Your Reader over the Head (5) _____ Beginning Hook (5)

_____Descriptive Attributes (5) _____Transitional Phrases (5)

_____Sentence Variation (5) _____Ending Technique (5)

Teacher Comments:

____

____

____

____

____

____

Sample Weighted Checklist for Expository Writing Process

Name:______________________________**Date:**______________**Score:**______________

_____Complete (60) _____ Body paragraphs (20)

_____ Prewriting (10) _____ Introductory paragraph and closing paragraph (10)

Teacher Comments:

____

____

____

____

____

____

CHAPTER SIX

Step Five—Revision and Editing

> Preparation for Publication

When students reread their work for the purposes of editing and revision, they are analyzing their own writing for quality and accuracy. Remind them that this is necessary before presenting anything "formal" to the public. Just like when they are dressing up for a special occasion, students will need to tend to all of the details that contribute to a quality presentation.

Most students do not readily dive into this part of the writing process. Once they have ideas on paper and conclusions written, they feel they are finished and do not want to revisit their writing. If you ask them to edit and revise their work they often finish rather quickly, having made few or no changes to their writing.

Before expecting students to reread in a critical fashion, tell them about your experiences with editing and revising. I invite my students to watch me when I write a note to a parent or an email to a colleague. I want them to observe the way I consciously reread my own writing and frequently make changes in even brief, informal messages.

I explain that if I am merely writing a reminder to myself, I am not so careful; however, if I am writing something that will be read by others, I want it to be perfect. I want to be sure my thoughts are expressed clearly and there are no mistakes in capitalization, punctuation, grammar, or spelling. If my message is of some length, I want to be sure it is enjoyable to read and will hold my reader's attention.

Stress that revision and editing are processes necessary to prepare a writer's work for public viewing. If someone else will be reading the piece, the writer must make sure it expresses ideas clearly, holds the reader's attention, and is free of inaccuracies.

> Revision and Editing with Target Skills

Students are at a loss when they are directed to "correct" their writing to "make it better." The consistent, precise language that comes from teaching with Target Skills allows teachers to specifically address composing and organizational skills that will prompt revisions and concretely address conventions that are necessary for editing.

Rather than addressing changes as whole, you will address individual Target Skills to help your students improve their writing. This will make the nebulous processes of revising and editing concrete and manageable for your students.

During revision and editing conferences, you should use the term "your reader" when suggesting changes: ***Your reader*** *will not know where sentences begin and end without end punctuation.* ***Your reader*** *will appreciate the addition of descriptive attributes in this passage.* ***Your reader*** *needs more specificity.* This language directs young authors to consider their audience while keeping that audience anonymous.

> Assessment

You will assess the published pieces at the end of this lesson sequence based upon the particular skills you have taught and can expect students to include in their writing. Be sure the expectations are clearly set and communicated to the students at the beginning of the process. You can use either a rubric or a weighted checklist, detailing specific skills you plan to assess. On the rubric, the word "consistently" has been added for the evaluation of language conventions. Samples are provided on page 81.

You may also choose to give students a process grade if you want to conduct formative evaluations throughout the process. Formative evaluations can assess students' participation and effort in conducting peer conferences, revising and editing their work. Your goal is for students to gain the ability to review their own work critically and independently.

If students are going to learn the procedures, they must consistently apply the skills with a sense of quality and competency. If there is a flaw in the process, the quality of the work will suffer. This type of assessment can help you identify specific process difficulties.

For this process assessment, I would suggest using a rubric instead of a weighted checklist. You can have students assess their own effort and participation as well.
A sample rubric is included on page 82.

No matter which assessment choices you make, you should evaluate your students' pieces after they've had the opportunity to make careful, thoughtful revisions. Hold students accountable for accuracy in conventions and quality of composition.

At the end of this step, your students will have accomplished more than writing an expository piece. They will have learned a process for revision and editing which they can apply in future writing across the curriculum.

> The Lessons

The lessons in this final step are designed to dissect the revising and editing processes into specific, isolated steps. If students can learn a procedure for reviewing their work under your direction, they will be better equipped for independent critical review of their writing.

The first lesson leads you in facilitating peer conferences to identify focus and organization. Next, you will be conducting a guided review of isolated composing skills. After this review, students will need time to revise their pieces and meet in peer conferences to obtain feedback on the changes.

After revision, you will lead your students through a guided review of conventions in isolation—reading and rereading for one convention Target Skill each time. You will teach students to "murmur read," a procedure developed by Marcia Freeman to slow down the rate of reading and help the students *listen* to their writing.

Once students have successfully followed these steps, they will have papers that are filled with colors and markings. They will also have learned a set of procedures for revising and editing their work. These procedures include careful analysis of composing skills, peer feedback and murmur reading for isolated convention skills. They have accomplished more than revision and editing at this point—they have learned a set of skills to carry with them in future writing.

Lesson 1: Organizational Skills	Materials: Expository genre-block piece, highlighter, blank copy of a graphic organizer (see pages 89-92).	Objective: Students will analyze their writing for focus and organization.
Lesson 2: Composing Skills	Materials: Expository genre-block piece, highlighter	Objective: Students will analyze their writing for composing skills.
Lesson 3: Conventions	Materials: Expository genre-block piece, colored pen, or pencil	Objective: Students will edit their writing.
Lesson 4: Publishing	Materials: Expository genre-block piece	Objectives: Students will publish an expository piece.

As the teacher, you may make decisions that alter this schedule, like speeding the process up by creating homework assignments, combining lessons, or slowing the process down by extending lessons or taking more teacher control over conferences and feedback. These decisions should be based on your knowledge of your students and your schedule. However, the sequence of the lessons should remain the same.

Lesson 1: Organizational Skills

Objective: Students will analyze their writing for focus and organization.

Materials: Expository genre-block piece, copy of a graphic organizer (see pages 89-92).

Mini-Lesson (10-15 minutes)

The amount of modeling you should do for this lesson depends on the age of your students, their competency with the skills you've taught, and their level of independence. Use a literature model of a brief expository piece. Post a large copy of the graphic organizer on the board, or use an overhead projector. Read the piece aloud, pausing occasionally to think out loud about the focus, main idea, and supporting details. Highlight the main idea of each paragraph. Write the main idea on the graphic organizer. Begin finding details in the story and sort details onto the graphic organizer. Look for "left field sentences" that are off-topic and interrupt the flow of the piece. Your objective is to work backwards to uncover the system of organization used. Collectively determine the focus of the piece.

Workshop (10-15 minutes)

Students should use highlighters to begin marking their own expository pieces. They should highlight main ideas, write main ideas on the graphic organizer, and list supporting details beneath each main idea statement. If support is limited, students can revise to add details at this point. If "left field sentences" are detected, they should be omitted. Circulate, monitor, and assist as needed.

Response (15-20 minutes)

Pair students for peer conferences. Each partner is responsible for analyzing another student's writing and comparing the piece to the graphic organizer created by the writer during workshop. After analyzing and comparing, the reader should identify the focus (main message) of the piece and discuss the overall focus, support, and organization with the writer. Students should make at least one positive comment in addition to one or two suggestions for improving the focus, organization, or adequacy of support. Partners should switch roles and repeat the process. When you see that pairs are beginning to finish, encourage them to return to their seats and work on revisions. When you see that most pairs are finished, survey the group and ask volunteers to share insights gained from the peer conferences.

Modifications

- You can give partners a blank graphic organizer to use during the peer conferences. They can analyze each other's writing and create a graphic organizer to compare to the one made by the writer.
- If time is limited, you can divide this lesson into two parts, having students analyze their own pieces and make revisions one day, and allowing a peer to analyze the piece the next day, followed by time for revision.
- If you would like to increase the amount of feedback each student receives, you can conduct two peer conferences or allow students to conference in small groups.
- Mature students can highlight the main ideas and details without transferring them onto a graphic organizer.

Lesson 2: Composing Skills

Objective: Students will analyze their writing for composing skills.

Materials: Expository genre-block piece, highlighter

Mini-Lesson (20-25 minutes)

During this lesson, you will conduct your students in a guided review of isolated organizational and composing skills. The skills identified will be the same organizational and composing skills taught and clearly stated in the expectations and assessment of the genre-block piece. You will call out one composing skill at a time, and allow time for students to read through their pieces, highlighting examples of that composing skill. After a brief time, call on students at random and ask them to share one, two, or three examples of the skill from their writing. For example: *Highlight your beginning hook.* Pause. Call on individuals: *Tell us the type of beginning hook you used and then read it to us.* After sampling most of the class, move on to another skill. *Highlight each transitional phrase you find in your piece.* Pause. Call on individuals: *Share three transitional phrases you used in your piece.* Repeat this process with other skills, like descriptive attributes, specificity, and ending techniques, isolating one skill at a time.

Workshop (10-15 minutes)

Students should work to add, extend, or improve organizational and composing skills. Circulate, assist, read, and provide feedback during workshop.

Response (5 minutes)

Conduct a brief class discussion about improvements made during this lesson. If time allows, encourage students to share examples of changes they made to their writing.

Modifications

- If time is limited, revisions following the mini-lesson can be assigned as homework, with a brief response at the beginning of the next lesson.
- For additional motivation, you can tie a teacher response to Target Skills identified by students. For example, ringing a bell or making a collective vocal response can be an auditory affirmation of mastery when a student shares three examples of a specific skill.
- With intermediate students, you may find it motivational to make tally marks on the board for examples of the identified skills, keeping a running tally of class totals. Older students can count identified skills applied in their pieces and keep personal tallies and totals.
- As students share examples of identified skills, write the examples down and create a list that can serve as a meaningful class resource.
- Before moving on to the next step, you may want to allow your students one class period for making revisions after these two days of analysis and critical review.

Lesson 3: Conventions

Objective: Students will edit their writing.

Materials: Expository genre-block piece, colored pen or pencil

Mini-Lesson (20-25 minutes)

During this lesson, you will conduct a guided review of isolated conventions. The skills identified will be the same ones clearly stated in the expectations and assessment of the genre-block piece. You will call out one convention skill at a time and allow students to read through their pieces to ensure accuracy of that convention.

Teach students to "murmur read" their pieces. As they read, their lips should be moving and their voices should create a low hum in the classroom. Students should use colored pens or pencils to make corrections in conventions. For example: *Murmur read your piece to check for capitalization of proper nouns, sentence beginnings, and the word "I."* Pause and allow students to work. Move on to another convention. *This time, murmur read your paper to check end punctuation.* Students will read for accuracy of only one convention at a time. I always save spelling for the last convention. Direct students to circle words if they are not positive that the spelling is correct. As students finish at different times, they can take out dictionaries to check spelling.

Workshop (15-20 minutes)

Students should have dictionaries available for looking up and correcting misspelled words. Have them use the colored pens or pencils to make any other corrections needed. Keeping a thesaurus accessible is a great idea in case students want to elevate vocabulary or find alternatives for repeated words. Circulate, monitor, and assist.

Response (10 minutes)

If time allows as students finish, you can pair them up to have another set of eyes review their work for accuracy. When most or all of your students have finished this process, ask them to identify common error patterns they found in their writing. Review the editing procedures used and address the benefits of an objective reader. Discuss strategies for remembering conventions, and review the process of rereading a piece for isolated skills.

Modifications

- If time is limited, you can conduct the mini-lesson in class and have students complete the corrections as a homework assignment.
- You may want to have students pair up for formal editing conferences and read each other's work for response time.
- You may want to provide a checklist of the skills that should be accurate to support students as they work independently.
- If you would like, you can teach editing marks to students to assist them with identifying specific errors in their writing.
- With younger students, you can provide an editing checklist and allow them to take the assignment home as homework. Parents can sign that they have reviewed the work for accuracy.
- If your students have access to computers and printers in their homes, you may require them to publish this piece at home. However, if you would like for them to use a computer lab at school—or if you would like for students to hand-write the final copy under your supervision—continue to Lesson Four.

Lesson 4: Publishing

If you require your students to make a final, clean copy of their piece as homework, you can skip this lesson. For teachers who would like to have the final copy created under their supervision (or with school resources), you can conduct the final publication of the piece at school, as detailed in this lesson.

Objective: Students will publish their expository pieces.

Materials: Expository genre-block pieces

Mini-Lesson (5 minutes)

At this point, all final revisions and editing should be complete. Explain to students that they will now publish their pieces. During this class session, you can allow students to rewrite their pieces by hand or have them type them in your school's computer lab.

Workshop (30 minutes)

Students will work on typing or rewriting final, published copies of their expository pieces. Times will vary based on student age and proficiency, especially if typing. Plan your time accordingly.

Response (5 minutes)

Before printing or submitting a final copy, encourage students to murmur read for accuracy and then find a second reader to check their work for mistakes they may have missed.

> Optional Lesson Ideas

- Students should have all of the practice pieces they have written during this unit (and others) stored in their writers' notebooks. You can practice the revision and editing lessons on short pieces before moving on to the actual expository piece you wish to practice. You can also provide additional practice with these skills after you have completed the published piece by selecting short pieces from the writers' notebooks.
- At any point, if you determine that your students need additional feedback, you can provide opportunities for peer conferences or small-group discussions.
- If you would like to conference with each student prior to publication, be sure to schedule individual conferences. Young students and students with limited writing experience will greatly benefit from individual student-teacher conferences.
- Editing for conventions provides a good opportunity for the application of grammar skills. If there is a particular skill you have been teaching or reviewing, add it to your editing process for applied practice.

> After the Final Copy

Once all students have completed the final copy of their expository pieces, you must find a way to take them to the public. This completes the publication process. If the teacher is the only one exposed to the piece, "publication" would entail a very limited audience. There are many options for publishing. Some are listed below.

- Conduct an author's chair session, in which all students have a turn to read their pieces to the class. Feedback can be provided according to your specifications.
- Search Internet resources, local newspapers, and teacher magazines for contests and publication opportunities.
- Arrange to display student work in a central location, such as the school media center or office.
- Make arrangements with a nearby branch library to display student work.
- If the topic relates to a content area, mail copies to a related organization.
- Conduct modified author's chair sessions in small groups, and allow groups to select the pieces that should be read to the rest of the class.
- Create a book from all of the individual pieces and keep it in the classroom.

> Remember

Writing is built upon details. Before students begin to write any expository piece, the first step should always be to list details related to the topic. Organization is important, but it should emerge from the details.

Writing is a developmental process. Students of the same age and grade level will not possess the same skills and fluency in writing. Be aware of individual differences and provide differentiated instruction.

Writing is not one skill, but a set of many component skills. Explicitly teach these skills and allow students to practice them before requiring that these skills be applied in a formal writing piece that is to be assessed.

Writing is an expressive language process, just like speaking. Learning to write involves discussion and modeling. It's not always a quiet activity. Students need to be able to try new skills out orally before they try them out in writing.

Finally, writing is meaning-centered. Topics should be meaningful to students. Allow students to choose topics and look for ways to tie writing to topics that are important to your students. This could mean writing about a unit of study from a different content area, a current event, or a general subject of interest. Allow your students to invest themselves in their writing and they will readily acquire the skills you are working to teach.

Sample Rubric for Published Piece

Name:____**Date:**__________________________

Skills	**3** Applies skills competently, creatively, and consistently	**2** Applies skills competently and consistently.	**1** Attempts to apply skills.	**0** Does not attempt to apply skills.
This paper contains a clear focus and is organized in a clear, logical fashion.				
This paper contains well-crafted composing skills, including: *specificity, descriptive attributes, and sentence variation.*				
The following conventions are accurate in this paper: *spelling, capitalization, and end punctuation.*				

Sample Weighted Checklist for Published Piece

Name:__________________________________ **Date:**______________________________

_____ Complete (60)

_____ Focus (5)

_____ Organization (5)

_____ Sentence variation (5)

_____ Descriptive Attributes (5)

_____ Specificity (5)

_____ Spelling (5)

_____ Capitalization (5)

_____ End punctuation (5)

Total Score: _____

Teacher Comments:

Sample Rubric for Revising and Editing Process Skills

Name:____**Date:**_________________________

Processes	**3** Follows procedures and applies skills competently, appropriately, and creatively.	**2** Follows procedures and applies skills competently and appropriately.	**1** Attempts to follow procedures and apply skills.	**0** Does not follow procedures or apply skills.
Peer conferences: *on task, insightful comments, ability to receive feedback.*				
Revision: *on task, making quality revisions, identifying skills accurately.*				
Editing: *on task, accurate, attending to details.*				

Bibliography

Websites:

Schmidt, B. (1997). Mark Twain Quotations, Newspaper Collections, and Related Resources. Retrieved from http://www.twainquotes.com

Professional Books:

Freeman, Marcia S. *Building a Writing Community.* Gainesville, FL: Maupin House Publishing, 1995.

Freeman, Marcia S. *CraftPlus Curriculum Guides.* Gainesville, FL: Maupin House Publishing, 2006.

Freeman, Marcia S. *Listen to This: Developing an Ear for Expository.* Gainesville, FL: Maupin House Publishing, 1997.

Freeman, Marcia S. with Mitten, Luana K., and Chappell, Rachel M. *Models for Teaching Writing-Craft Target Skills.* Maupin House Publishing, 2005.

Keene, Ellin Oliver and Zimmerman, Susan *Mosaic of Thought.* Portsmouth, NH: Heinemann, 1997.

Trade Books:

Freedman, Russell. *Lincoln: A Photobiography.* New York, NY: Clarion Books, 1987: 13-14.

Paulsen, Gary. *Father Water, Mother Woods: Essays on Fishing and Hunting in the North Woods.* New York, NY: Delacorte Press, 1994: 105.

Truman, Margaret. *First Ladies*, New York, NY: Random House, 1995.

APPENDIX A

A Brief Overview of the CraftPlus® Curriculum

The teaching methods and concepts presented in this book are based on the principles and practices of CraftPlus®, an approach to writing instruction that was developed by Marcia S. Freeman.

CraftPlus instruction is a curriculum built upon the explicit teaching of writing craft, presented as isolated Target Skills®. Target Skills® are modeled and directly taught. Students are provided with ample practice and support as they develop facility with Target Skills. The ultimate goal is for students to apply these writing-craft skills competently and creatively in their written work.

> CraftPlus Principles

- The writing process is what writers *do*; writing craft is what writers *know.*
- Writing craft is a set of specific organizational, composing and convention skills.
- Writing should be viewed as an academic subject that is explicitly taught.
- Like all effective teaching, writing-craft instruction should proceed from simple to complex, and from concrete to abstract.
- CraftPlus emphasizes non-fiction, which encompasses most of our required writing.
- CraftPlus links writing to reading with the use of literature models, which builds and reinforces both language processes.

> CraftPlus Practices

- Lessons are focused on specific Target Skills.
- Writing is taught using models from printed works and student writing.
- Composing and convention skills are applied across genres.
- Organizational strategies are taught as genre-specific processes.
- Genre-specific writing-craft skills are taught and applied in genre blocks.
- Student writing assignments consist of 85% practice and 15% assessment.
- Writing instruction is conducted in a daily writing workshop environment tied to short, focused mini-lessons.
- Traditional writing process strategies are modified to include procedures for peer response, revision and editing.
- Revision is emphasized. Teaching with Target Skills gives students specific revision goals.
- Student writers maintain personal writers' notebooks. Teachers maintain instructional notebooks or files.
- Writing assessment is objective, focusing on specific organizational, composing, or convention skills.

> A Sample of Target Skills

Organizational	Composing	Conventions
• Listing • Transitions • Beginning Techniques • Graphic Organizers • Sorting/classifying • Ending Technique • Ordering • Establishing Focus • Paragraph sStructures	• Specificity • Dialogue • Voice • Clues for Inference • Supporting Detail Types • Literary Devices	• Punctuation • Capitalization • Grammar

>Methodology

CraftPlus lessons are based on teaching craft through Target Skills and modeling. Lessons generally follow this sequence:

- Expose students to a new Target Skill by using a literature model.
- Discuss the skill or technique.
- Model the use of the skill, both orally and in writing.
- Allow students to practice the skill, first orally and then in writing.
- Provide opportunities for practice with lots of encouragement and feedback, along with supplementary modeling and instruction.
- Finally, assess students' mastery of the Target Skill in a required written piece.

> Lesson Plans

Teachers who implement the CraftPlus curriculum maintain instructional notebooks or files, which continue to grow from year to year with additional lesson plans, models, assessment options and teaching ideas.

A lesson plan follows this general order:

1. Objective (Target Skill)
2. Genres to which the Target Skill can be applied
3. Time parameters
4. Materials
5. Literature models
6. Procedure: Mini-lesson, Workshop, Response, Follow-up lessons

> Models

Target Skills should always be presented in models. Models can be collected from literature, textbooks, magazines, student work, and teacher composition.

Models should be brief, focused and well-crafted. If you wish to model a non-example (a poor application) of a Target Skill, create that model yourself. Never use a student's work as a non-example.

Save models in your writing instruction notebook or files. As years go by, your resources will grow.

> Genre Blocks

A genre block is a period of time you devote to instruction in a specific genre. This book presents lessons for a thorough expository genre block. Over the course of the genre block, skills are explicitly taught and practiced.

Select skills from each set: organizational, composing and conventions. Students in fourth through tenth grades can handle several Target Skills during a genre block. Some skills are usually review skills, while others are new skills.

After teaching the set of skills you have designed for any genre block, plan a writing piece which requires students to apply those skills. During the last few days of the genre block, provide instruction in revising and editing. Allow students to practice these skills as they polish and refine their composition.

> Assessment

Because Target Skills are focused and specific, assessment can be objective. Use a single-skill rubric for assessing mastery of a single Target Skill. Use the multiple-skill assessment rubric for assessing multiple Target Skills or a genre-block writing piece. If you need to attain a percentage, you can use a weighted checklist for assessing a writing piece.

No matter which instrument you use, assessing Target Skills should be directly tied to instruction. Use assessments to evaluate mastery and determine specific needs for re-teaching and remediation.

> Remember

CraftPlus principles are consistent with current educational theory and practice. Instruction is direct and explicit. Modeling is at the heart of instruction. Skills are taught in a systematic manner, progressing from simple to complex and from concrete to abstract.

Students are provided with ample practice and assessment is authentic and tied to instruction. The curriculum emphasizes non-fiction writing, which accounts for the bulk of writing that will be required of students in their adult and professional lives.

APPENDIX B
Reproducibles

Types of Supporting Details with Examples

Specific or concrete examples:

Many foods are rich in calcium, like milk, yogurt, cheese, and even broccoli!

Facts:

Many companies are beginning to eliminate trans-fats from their packaged foods.

Self-evident truths:

Good health is the product of good habits.

Anecdotes (narrative vignettes):

Once when I was younger, I ate a chocolate bar for breakfast. I became hungry within an hour of my "breakfast" and by mid-morning I was irritable and unable to concentrate.

Comparison or Analogies:

Foods high in carbohydrates produce a sudden burst of energy, but foods rich in protein provide a more durable, longer lasting source of energy.

Authoritative Quotes or Testimonials:

In the words of my dentist, "Don't be in a rush when you brush."

Numbers/Statistics:

Seventy-five percent of Americans begin their new year with a resolution involving healthy habits.

Descriptive Details:

The brown, fuzzy exterior of the kiwi is a contrast to its sweet, juicy, bright green interior.

Definition:

"Triglycerides" is the scientific name for fats that can travel in your bloodstream.

Graphic Organizer: Boxed Flow Chart

Topic and Focus:

Topic / Ending Technique:

Graphic Organizer: Concept Boxes

Topic/Focus:____

Concept #1:	Concept #2:	Concept #3:

Graphic Organizer: Concept Web

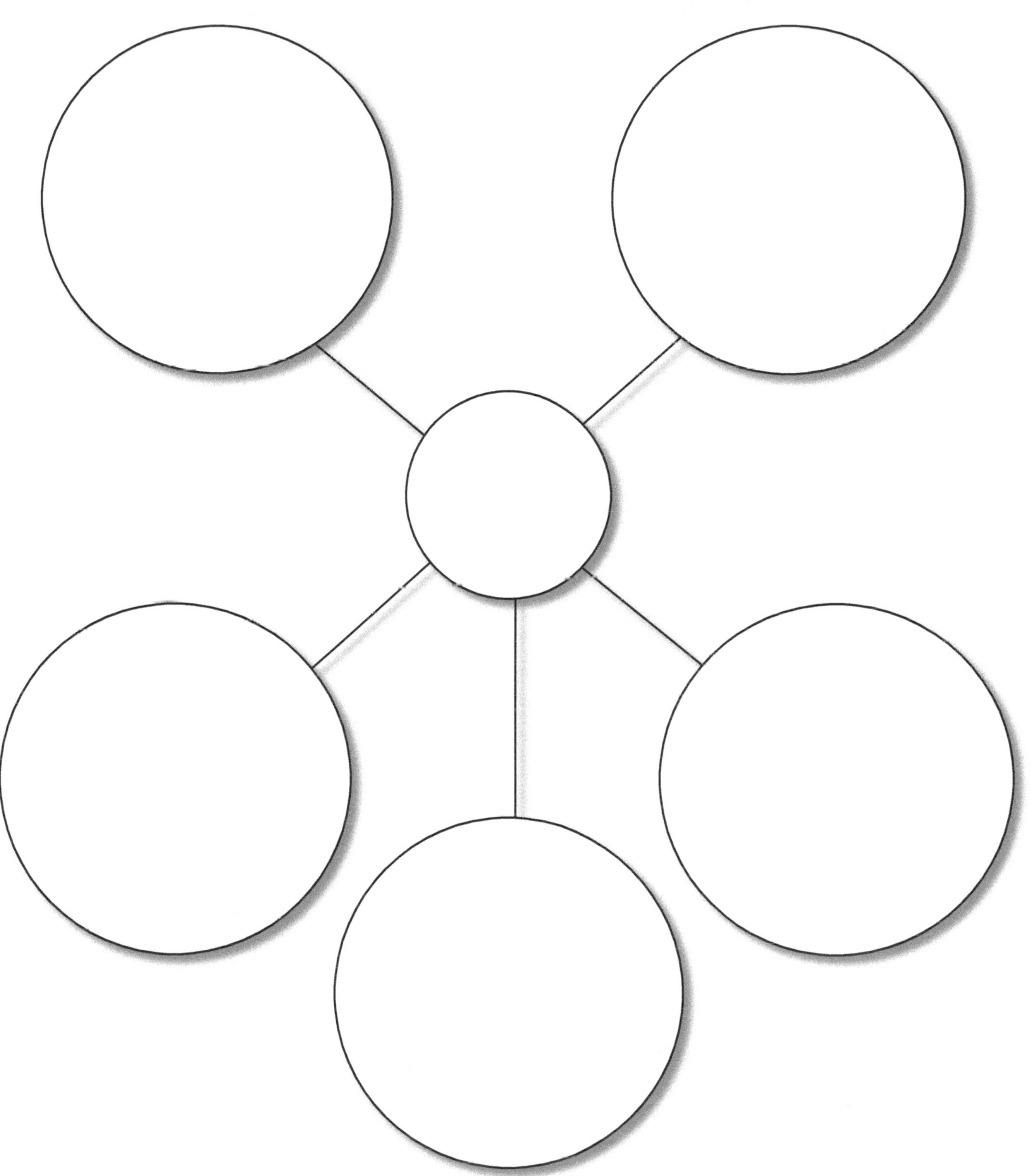

Graphic Organizer: Outline

Topic and Focus:____

I.____

1.
2.
3.
4.
5.

II.____

1.
2.
3.
4.
5.

III.____

1.
2.
3.
4.
5.

Topic and Ending Technique:_________________________________

____

____

____

____

____

Process Paper: How to Upholster a Chair

By Lana Middlebrooks
Used with permission

Decorating your house can be difficult and expensive. One way to save money is to upholster your furniture yourself. Given good instructions, you can beautify your home and bask in the pride of doing it yourself. First, if you realize that you have difficulty choosing colors that complement one another, ask a friend who has good taste for advice. Visit her home, and confirm her skills. Next, you must measure the piece of furniture to be covered; be sure to write these numbers in a secure place so as to avoid appearing foolish at the fabric store. As soon as possible, choose your fabric, remembering to take your talented friend along. Purchase the material, then stop by the hardware store and buy an electric staple gun and some protective glasses. Pick up an extra pair for your friend. By this time she has been coerced into helping you. Next, lay the fabric on a solid, flat surface such as a kitchen table, and carefully cut the cloth into the desired dimensions. Meanwhile, your friend is extricating the seat from the chair that is to be covered. You have fed her a lovely lunch, which has banished all hostility provoked by having been tricked into helping you. After the cloth is cut, place it on the area to be covered, making sure that all sides are even. Put on the protective eyewear and ask that your friend do the same. Load the staples into the electric stapler and plug it in. Afterward, hold down the fabric, aim the stapler, and staple the fabric into place. Repeat this process for all corners. Next, after having checked for injuries, reattach the covered piece to the chair. Finally, invite friends and family over to admire your skills and give you numerous compliments. As soon as possible, purchase a gift for your generous friend, and allow a credible amount of time to pass before you ask her to do this again. Enjoy!

Beginning Hooks with Examples

Question: *Do you value your freedom so much that you would be willing to sacrifice your life to preserve it?*

Onomatopoeia: *Kaching! The cash register will be overflowing once my business is up and running.*

Exclamations: *Eureka! Discovering a new fishing hole can be as exciting as finding gold.*

Startling fact: *At least 37.5 million acres of rainforest are destroyed each year.*

Voice: *Are you looking for a tasty snack that's low in fat and packed with vitamins? Well, have I got a treat for you!*

Definition: *Alopecia Areata is an autoimmune disease in which the immune system mistakenly attacks hair follicles, causing hair loss that can range from moderate to extensive.*

General to specific statement: *Most of us have at least one hero or source of inspiration. For me, that hero is Eleanor Roosevelt.*

Riddle: *Can you name a mammal that has two layers of fur, webbed feet, a duck-bill and a habit of laying eggs?*

Quotation: *"If the Union was to be saved, it had to be a man of such an origin that should save it." These are the immortal words of Mark Twain, written about Abraham Lincoln and his humble origins.*

Anecdote: *According to Margaret Truman's* First Ladies, *when George Washington first became president, he allowed callers to visit his home unannounced. After weeks of getting very little governmental business accomplished due to an overwhelming number of social calls, Washington limited visitors to two hours per week. In ways great and small, Washington shaped the role of the president.*

Idiom: *The early bird catches the worm. If you want to find the best deals at garage sales, you'd better heed this advice.*

Sentence fragments: *A Trojan horse. That's one way to describe the duplicity of a double agent.*

Paragraph Assessment Grid

Class________________________

Student	Comparison	Deductive	Inductive	Cause/ Effect	Question/ Answer	Introduction	Conclusion

Descriptive Attributes with Examples

Action: crawl, slide, skip, saunter, amble, promenade

Size: immense, miniscule, diminutive, four-by-four inches

Color: pale green, ghostly white, soft yellow, grayish

Shape: oval, triangular, elliptical, pear-shaped, angular

Texture: fuzzy, smooth, rough, jagged, bumpy

Smell: putrid, acrid, fragrant, burnt, vanilla-scented

Taste: bitter, fruity, tangy, salty, sweet, sour, zesty

Sound: piercing, high-pitched, grating, melodious

Composition: wooden, concrete, felt, synthetic, organic

Character: honest, loyal, frugal, polite, even-tempered, volatile

Weather: balmy, humid, frigid, cool, stormy

Emotional: nervous, anxious, jovial, jealous, shy

Physical: towering, lanky, gawky, statuesque, bony, slender

Tempo: quick, adagio, fast-paced, moderate, allegretto

Movement: agile, clumsy, cat-like, stilted, fluid, awkward

Behavior: rude, oafish, attentive, civil, gracious, uncouth

Sample Expository Prompts

Each of us has at least one person whom we greatly admire and respect. Think of someone you admire and respect. Write to explain why you admire and respect this person.

We are often told that regular exercise is essential to good health. Write to explain why regular exercise is essential to good health.

Holiday observations are important across various cultures. Think of a holiday that is important to you. Write to explain how you observe this particular holiday.

Think of a vacation spot you would like to visit. Write to explain why you would like to visit this vacation destination.

Writing is an important form of communication. Explain to your reader how to write in a way that is clear and enjoyable to read.

Writing is an important form of communication. Write to explain why it is important to learn to write in a way that is clear and enjoyable to read.

We all have favorite hobbies and pastimes. Think of your favorite hobby or pastime. Write to explain why you enjoy this activity.

Most of us have a personal area of expertise. Write to provide information about your particular area of expertise.

Consider the rules students must follow at your school. Write to explain why these rules are important.

Think of a game you enjoy playing. Write to tell the reader how this game is played.

The weather can have both positive and negative affects on our plans and activities. Write to explain how the weather can impact your plans in both positive and negative ways.

Many school cafeterias are undergoing renovations to make their food choices and atmospheres more appealing to students. Write to tell the reader about changes you think should be made in your school cafeteria. Provide reasons why you think these changes are needed.

Friends are important parts of our lives. Think of the qualities you look for in a good friend. Write to tell the reader about these qualities of a good friend and explain why you think they are important.

"Don't Hit Your Reader over the Head" Activity Cards

He looked sad.	She was nervous.	It was hot.
He was scared.	It was a beautiful day.	Everyone was surprised.
It was a quiet night.	The town was small.	The music was loud.
The food was good.	We had fun at the fair.	It was a long ride.
I am hungry.	He is tall.	She is honest.
The circus is exciting.	He is polite.	The snow was cold.
Raking leaves is hard work.	I was tired.	That baby is fussy.
I like pizza.	The pool is cold.	She looked busy.
She was embarrassed.	The crowd was disappointed.	That house is big.
My brother is annoying.	That dog is vicious.	That dog is cute.

Single-Skill Assessment Rubric

Name: ____ Date:_____________________

Target Skill	Score:
Applies Target Skill creatively and competently.	3
Applies Target Skill competently.	2
Attempts to apply Target Skill.	1
Makes no attempt to apply Target Skill.	0

Teacher Comments: ____

____

____

Name: ____ Date:_____________________

Target Skill	Score:
Applies Target Skill creatively and competently.	3
Applies Target Skill competently.	2
Attempts to apply Target Skill.	1
Makes no attempt to apply Target Skill.	0

Teacher Comments: ____

____

____

Name: ____ Date:_____________________

Target Skill	Score:
Applies Target Skill creatively and competently.	3
Applies Target Skill competently.	2
Attempts to apply Target Skill.	1
Makes no attempt to apply Target Skill.	0

Teacher Comments: ____

____

____

Multiple-Skill Assessment Rubric

Name: ________________________________ Date: ______________________

Target Skills	**3** Applies Target Skill creatively and competently.	**2** Applies Target Skill creatively.	**1** Attempts to apply Target Skill.	**0** Makes no attempt to apply Target Skill.
Organizational Skill(s):				
Composing Skill(s):				
Convention(s):				

Teacher Comments: ____

____

____

Name: ________________________________ Date: ______________________

Target Skills	**3** Applies Target Skill creatively and competently.	**2** Applies Target Skill creatively.	**1** Attempts to apply Target Skill.	**0** Makes no attempt to apply Target Skill.
Organizational Skill(s):				
Composing Skill(s):				
Convention(s):				

Teacher Comments: ____

____

____

Expository Genre-Block Planning Tool

Grades 4-10

_____**General Expository** _____**Process Paper**

- o Self-Selected Topic
- o Prompt:____
- o Picture Prompt:____
- o Content-Area Piece:____

Literature Models:

_________________________________ _________________________________

_________________________________ _________________________________

Graphic Organizer:

_____Boxed Flow Chart
_____Concept Boxes
_____Concept Web
_____Outline

Assessment:

_____Multiple-Skill Rubric
_____Weighted Checklist
_____Other:___________________________

Target Skill Choices

Organizational Skills	Conventions

Composing Skills

Notes:

____
____
____

CraftPlus® COMPARISON ANALYSIS ORGANIZER

ATTRIBUTE	X	BOTH	Y

APPENDIX C
Student Samples

Student Sample: Expository Detail List

(by Chad, Grade 4)

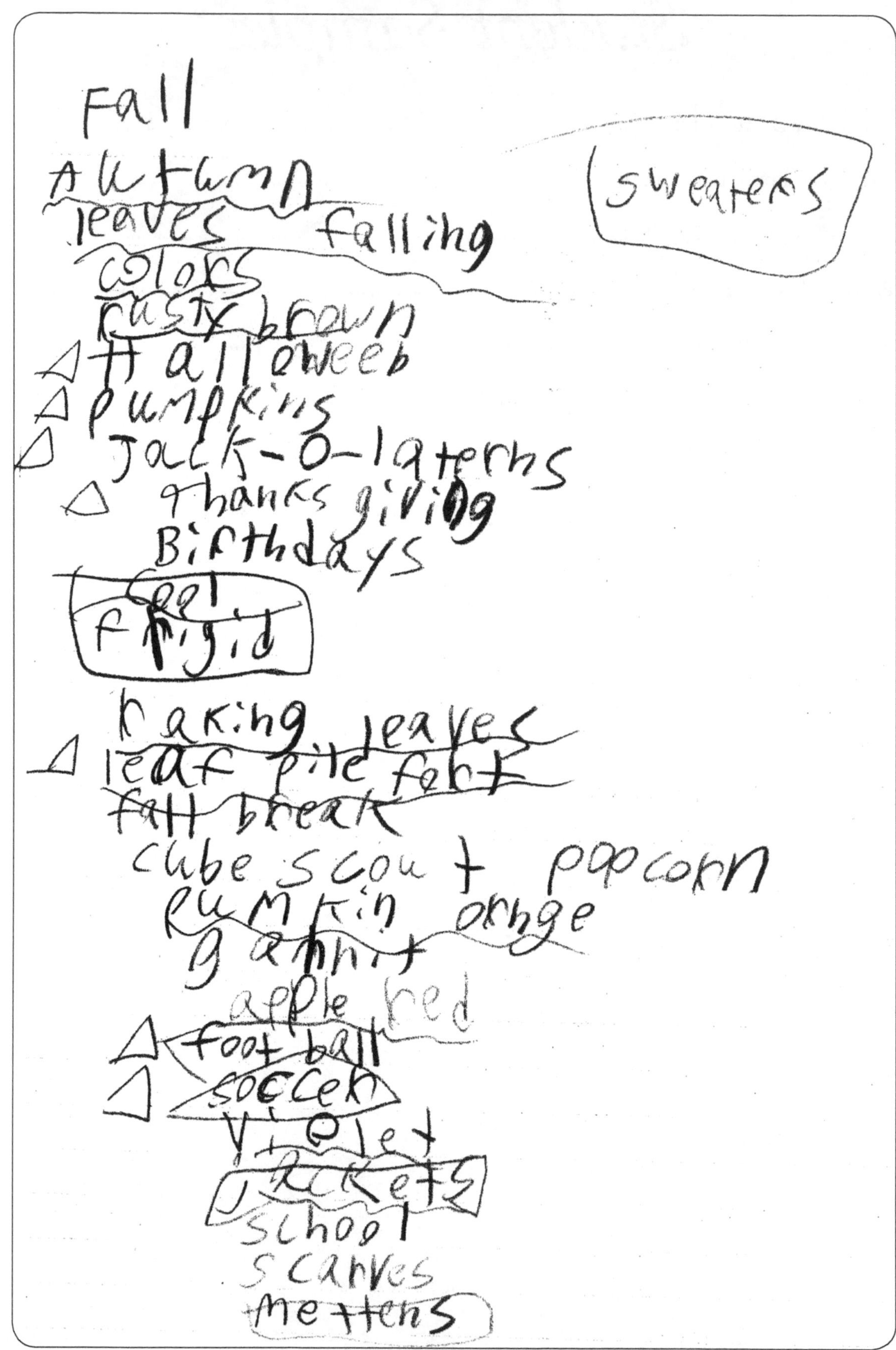

Fall

Autumn

leaves falling

colors

rusty brown

Halloween

pumpkins

Jack-o-laterns

thanks giving

Birthdays

cool

frigid

raking leaves

leaf pile fort

fall break

cube scout + popcorn

pumkin orange

garnit

apple red

football

soccer

violet

jackets

school

scarves

mettens

sweaters

Student Sample: Organizer: Boxed Flow Chart

(by Chad, Grade 4)

Student Sample: Types of Supporting Details

(by Cody, Grade 4)

Let me indroduce myself. My name is Cody. I am GOOD at football. I hit Some body so hard they dropped the ball and I scord a tuch down. I have scorde 250 points worth of tuch downs and field goals. Somebody said, "You play like a young snake." One time I scored 17 points fore the "bulldogs". Some Day my goal is to play on th Rams.

Student Sample: Process Plan and Paragraph

(by Dylan, Grade 10)

HOW TO: make a smoothie

gather materials.

get out the blender and put in 4 pieces of ice. Then add fruits, (strawberries, bananas, etc.)

then add sugar.

after that pour 1 1/2 cups of milk and/or yogurt.

turn blender on.

mix it up.

then pour, and enjoy.

"Yum! This smoothie is delicious, and nutricious!" Many people enjoy drinking smoothies, but do you know how to make them? Well, first off you get out the blender and fruits, and the liquids. Then you put 4 pieces of ice in the blender. After that, you add "the fruits". This can be strawberries, bananas, rasberries, etc. Then you add as much sugar as you think you need. After you add the sugar, you pour in milk, 1 1/2 cups to be exact. You can also add vanilla yogurt, if you would like to. Then you turn on the blender and mix these items together. Turn the blender off, and serve in various cups and enjoy.

Student Sample: Comparison Paragraph and Comparison Organizer

(by Shelby, Grade 7)

Cats and dogs have many things that are alike and many things that are diffrant. Somethings that are the same are, how Dogs and cats both have furr all over their bodies. A nother simalarity is Cats and Dogs both walk on four legs. But, I think the bigest diffrence is the sounds they make. Cats meow, while dogs bark. So, They might be alike or diffrant but eather way cats and dogs are very special.

NAME: Shelby

DATE: 2/20/07

ATTRIBUTE	CATS	BOTH	DOGS
Fur		all over their bodys	
Walk		on all four legs	
Sounds	They Meow		They bark or Woof

Student Sample: Deductive and Inductive Paragraph Forms

(by Emily, Grade 9)

Winter is here.

Specific Details:

- Crisp Air
- Holidays
- Leafless Trees
- Cold Weather
- Frost

Deductive Paragraph

Winter seems to be taking its course, can you tell? As I step out into the now frigid weather, my lungs are ablaze with the crisp air. Leafless trees line the streets. Frost is no stranger as it gingerly coats rooftops. Lights on every house serve as a reminder that the holiday season is approaching. Winter is in the air.

Inductive Paragraph

Jingle, Jangle! Jingle, Jangle! The Holiday season truly fills the room. We all stay inside to keep warm, but that's alright with us. Everytime we go outside, the frost has covered something new! The car, the roof, the toys, you name it, it's frosted! But it's all from the same cause, winter is here!

Student Sample: Five-Paragraph Expository Paper (Rough Draft)

(by Luke, Grade 4)

Dear children, let us get back to the tale of our country. After a very rough fight called the Revolutionary War, the thirteen colonies became the U.S.A. (United States of America) and a new country was born. The US was starting to expand, and more and more people set up homes there. IF a certain discovery hadn't been made to bring people west, America might be as cramped as England!

Now their was this man named John Sutter, who had a dream of owning a farming empire. When he became a citizen of Mexico, his dream came true when he bought land for a place called 'Sutter's Fort.' In fact, more than 200 Mormons sailed to the part of land where Sutter's Fort was, many getting jobs working there. In 1848, almost 300 people were at Sutters Fort, which made a sawmill very vital to the fort's survival. A man named James Marshall who was hired to build this sawmill

near part of the American River. As he had been walking in a ditch, he saw the glint of shiny pebbles. They were yellowish, they were - GOLD! He had found **GOLD**!!!
Though he tried to keep it a secret, it was too hard! Soon, a newspaper called the California star came out with a special edition all about the gold. But soon the publisher of star, Sam Brannan, found out the only way to start the gold rush was to see gold. He went prospecting him-self and found gold dust! He displayed it to many people shouting "GOLD! GOLD! GOLD! FROM THE AMERICAN RIVER!!!" In just three days, four hundred people left their homes to mine gold. But the rush still hadn't began. Only when president James Polk verified that the gold was real had the gold rush began. In 1849, everyone was looking for gold.

new paragraph → Children, you now know the tale of how the California gold rush started.

Student Sample: Five-Paragraph Expository Paper—Edited and Revised

(by Alayna, Grade 4)

Gumbo

"How about trying new foods for once? It can't possibly hurt you!" That's what my mom said as she held a spoonful of steaming hot, brown Gumbo in front of my face with me refusing to taste it. But I just didn't know how good it actually was.

My poor, dear mother tried practically everything to get me to eat Gumbo. From the cheesiest to the sneakiest. She told me it was yummy. Since I was also a mini-me of my big sister, she told me, "but your sister eats it." She said I would regret it if I didn't eat it. She tried to sneak the spoon into my mouth, and she begged and pleaded. None of it worked. It was both sneaky and cheesy. What got me to eat Gumbo was her saying that the rice was a special type of ice cream and the brown stuff was chocolate.

Once I found out, I absolutely loved it. I would ask my mom what made Gumbo so delectable. I was only 5 so I was too young to understand a real recipe. So she told me it was magic gumbo beans. I'm crazy about it so much that I want you to try it. I promise you will like it. Why not try it? It's delicious. It is good on a cold winter's night, it's spicy and it's mouth watering just for me to talk about it. It will give you the best night's sleep you ever had, I guarantee.

Unlike most foods, Gumbo has a gargantuan history behind it. Gumbo comes from African words meaning Okra. The way Gumbo started was when the first French settlers went to Louisiana they brought their love for some famous French stew known as Bouillabaisse. Since both my parents were born in Louisiana and my family originated in France, the Gumbo recipe is kind of a pass it down thing. Gumbo is a stew that is especially important on a holiday called Mardi Gras (AKA: Fat Tuesday).

In areas of Louisiana they have a run of Mardi Gras. That's when a group of masked and costumed horseback riders go to different houses and ask for permission to come inside, and once permission is granted they dance, sing, and beg for one ingredient of Gumbo. A lot of times the owner of the house will throw a chicken up in the air and they will run after it like football players. There are many different ways to make Gumbo, but the kind we usually make has these ingredients: okra, chicken, water, green onion, parsley, garlic, salt, pepper, bell pepper, celery, sausage, shrimp, roux, and it is served over rice. And Voila! Yummy Gumbo! Good thing my mom finally got me to eat Gumbo. Won't you try it? As my mom said, "it can't possibly hurt you."

Notes:

Notes:

Notes:

Notes: